Lewis F. Lindsay

Hymn-Songs

For Use in the Sunday School, Young People's Meeting, the Church....

Lewis F. Lindsay

Hymn-Songs

For Use in the Sunday School, Young People's Meeting, the Church....

ISBN/EAN: 9783337089771

Printed in Europe, USA, Canada, Australia, Japan

Cover: Foto ©Thomas Meinert / pixelio.de

More available books at **www.hansebooks.com**

HYMN-SONGS

FOR USE IN

The Sunday School,

Young People's Meeting,

The Church and Home.

SELECTED BY

LEWIS F. LINDSAY, and JAS N. CLEMMER.

MUSICAL EDITORS:

JOHN R. SWENEY, and WM. J. KIRKPATRICK.

PHILADELPHIA:

John J. Hood,

1024 Arch Street.

Copyright, 1895, by JOHN J. HOOD.

Price, board covers, 35 cents per copy, mailed; $3 60 per dozen, at store.

HYMN-SONGS.

Gloria Patri.

CHARLES MEINEKE.

Glo-ry be to the Father, and to the Son, and to the Ho-ly Ghost, as it was in the be-gin-ning, is now, and ev-er shall be, world without end. A-men, a-men.

Doxology.

Tune, OLD HUNDRED. L. M.

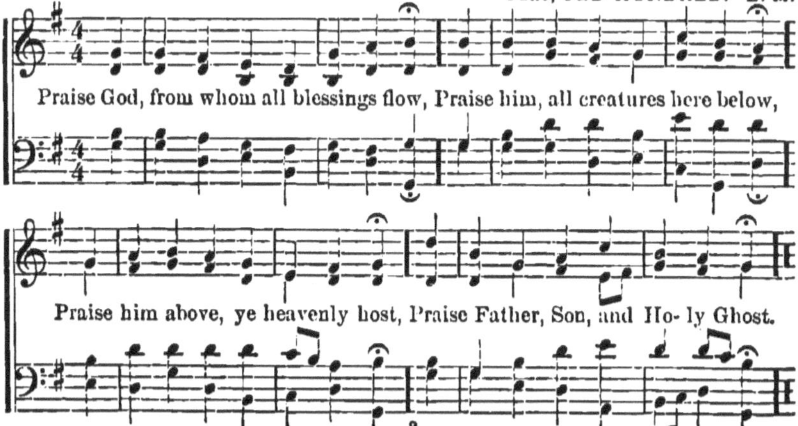

Praise God, from whom all blessings flow, Praise him, all creatures here below, Praise him above, ye heavenly host, Praise Father, Son, and Ho-ly Ghost.

The Future.—CONCLUDED.

know . . not where I'll be, But where'er - - my path be
future lies before me, And I know not where I'll be, But where'er my path be leading, Saviour,

lead - - ing, Saviour, keep . . . my heart with thee.
keep my heart with thee, But where'er my path be leading, Saviour, keep my heart with thee.

Heaven is My Home.

SCOTCH MELODY.

mf Adagio e Legato.

1. { I'm but a stranger here, Heav'n is my home; }
   { Earth is a desert drear, Heav'n is my home; } Danger and sorrow stand

2. { What tho' the tempest rage? Heav'n is my home; }
   { Short is my pilgrimage, Heav'n is my home; } Time's cold and wintry blast

Round me on ev'ry hand; Heav'n is my Fatherland, Heav'n is my home.
Soon will be o-verpast; I shall reach home at last; Heav'n is my home.

3 Peace! O my troubled soul,
Heav'n is my home;
I soon shall reach the goal;
Heav'n is my home;
Swiftly the race I'll run,
Yield up my crown to none;
Forward! the prize is won;
Heav'n is my home.

4 There, at my Saviour's side,
Heav'n is my home;
I shall be glorified;
Heav'n is my home;
There are the good and blest,
Those I loved most and best,
There, too, I soon shall rest,
Heav'n is my home.

10. Salvation's River.

R. Kelso Carter.   S. C. Foster.

1. Down at the cross, on Calvary's mountain, Where mer-cies flow,
When nothing in the whole cre-a-tion Could purchase peace,
I plunged in the redeem-ing fountain, Washed whiter than the snow.
My Saviour brought his free salva-tion, Gave me complete re-lease.

CHORUS.
Broth-ers, wont you hear the sto-ry? See the fount-ain flow!
Oh, glo-ry in the highest, glo-ry! Je-sus saves me, this I know.

Copyright, 1889.—Property of John J. Hood.

2 When lost in sin, my all I squandered,
   Far from the fold:
My Saviour sought me where I wandered,
   Gave me his wealth untold.
All bonds of sin and Satan rending,
   Christ made me whole:
I'll ne'er forget that joy transcending,
   When Jesus saved my soul.

3 All round my way the sun is shining,
   Darkness has fled:
On Jesus' breast I am reclining,
   Daily by him I'm fed.
My Lord has cast his robe around me,
   No more I'll roam;
The Shepherd of the sheep has found me,
   Jesus has brought me home.

The New Jerusalem. 11

"*Our feet shall stand within thy gates, O Jerusalem.*"

Rev. Wm. H. Hunter, D. D.
Jno. R. Sweney.

1. Je-ru-sa-lem! thy mansions fair Ig-noble souls may never share;
   For all who walk thy streets of gold Are in the book of life en-roll'd.
2. Who-so from earth would thither go, Must wash his robes as white as snow;—
   In Je-sus' blood, the fount of grace, Find pure, unspotted righteousness.

CHORUS.
O, Je-ru-sa-lem! Blessed Jeru-sa-lem! Our feet with-in thy gates shall stand! O, Je-ru-sa-lem! New Je-ru-sa-lem!

3 O Lamb of God, my heart prepare,
  To enter with the holy there;
  Within thy book my name enroll,
  And write thine own upon my soul.

4 To him that loves and trusts the Lord,
  And keeps with patient hope his word,
  The Spirit with his spirit bears
  Sweet witness to his answered prayers.

5 Whoever has this seal of love
  His title reads to seats above;
  And looking upward as he runs,
  The taint of sinful pleasure shuns.

6 Jesus, fulfil my long desire
  To stand with thee in pure attire,
  And find at last a place and name
  Within the New Jerusalem.

Copyright, 1877, by JOHN J. HOOD.

Then Rejoice, all Ye Ransomed. 13

"There is joy in the presence of the angels of God, over one sinner that repenteth." Luke xv. 10.

E. F. M. E. F. MILLER.

1. There's re-joicing in the presence of the an-gels O-ver
2. Oh, how happy is the sinner who has tast-ed Of the
3. In the home where once was strife and pain and sorrow, There'll be
4. We will ral-ly round the standard of our Sav-iour, And to

sinners coming home, . All the heav'nly harpers, with a mighty
Saviour's wond'rous love, Love that bringeth peace and joy, which passeth
blessed peace and joy, . Prayer and praise to God around the family
oth-ers loud-ly call, . Come, ye sinners, and repent, believe in

D. S.—dead's alive, the lost is found, and
Fine. CHORUS.

chorus, Now are praising round the throne. Then rejoice, . . all ye
knowledge, Ever giv-en from a-bove.
al-tar Will the pow'r of sin destroy.
Je-sus, He will freely pardon all.

wand'rers Now are coming, coming home.

D. S.

ran-somed, Let your praises reach to heaven's highest dome, For the

From the "Shout of Victory By per."

Rest Ever With God.—CONCLUDED. 15

shore, With the holy Church Triumphant there To rest ever with God.

Wonderful Peace.

L. H. E.   "My peace I give unto you."—John xiv: 27.   L. H. EDMUNDS.

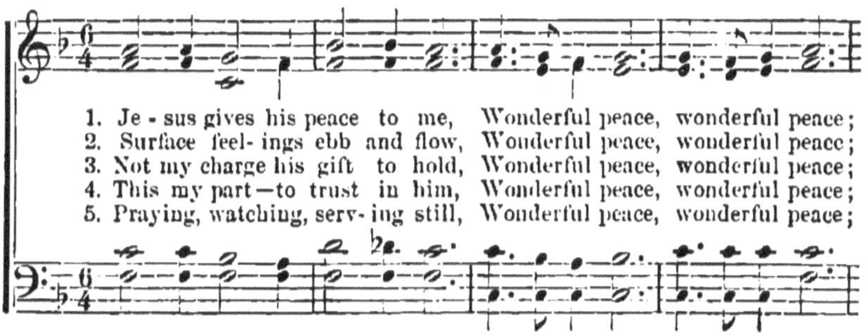

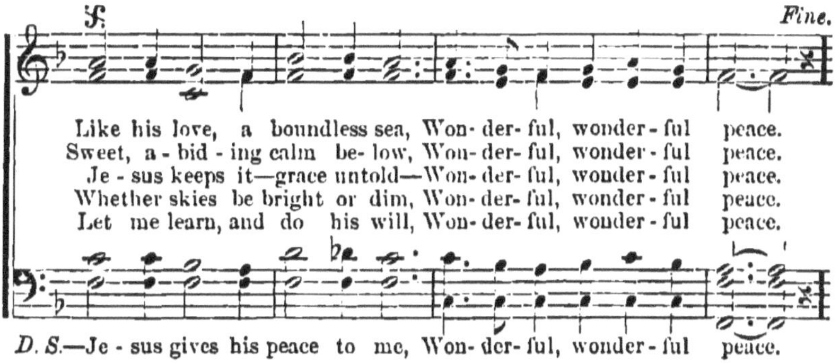

1. Je - sus gives his peace to me, Wonderful peace, wonderful peace;
2. Surface feel- ings ebb and flow, Wonderful peace, wonderful peace;
3. Not my charge his gift to hold, Wonderful peace, wonderful peace;
4. This my part—to trust in him, Wonderful peace, wonderful peace;
5. Praying, watching, serv- ing still, Wonderful peace, wonderful peace;

S.   *Fine.*

Like his love, a boundless sea, Won- der- ful, wonder- ful peace.
Sweet, a - bid - ing calm be- low, Won- der- ful, wonder- ful peace.
Je - sus keeps it—grace untold—Won- der- ful, wonder- ful peace.
Whether skies be bright or dim, Won- der- ful, wonder- ful peace.
Let me learn, and do his will, Won- der- ful, wonder- ful peace.

D. S.—Je - sus gives his peace to me, Won- der- ful, wonder- ful peace.

REFRAIN.   *D.S.*

Peace, peace, won - der - ful peace, Peace, peace, won - der - ful peace;

Copyright, 1886, by John J. Hood.

Oh, such Wonderful Love! 19

I. N. McH.   I. N. McHose.

1. O the great love the dear Saviour has shown To shamefully die on the tree,
2. Palaces, mansions, and inns had no room For Christ, who so joyfully came
3. Man of great sorrows and homeless was he, But yet my Redeemer and Friend,

Leaving his sceptre and beautiful throne To rescue a sin- ner like me!
Down from yon heaven our path to illume, And save us from sin and from shame.
Pouring in infinite streams upon me, A love that can nevermore end.

CHORUS.

Oh, ... such wonderful love, Oh, ... such wonderful love;
Oh, such wonder- ful,   Oh, such wonder- ful,

Jesus my Saviour left sceptre and throne, To rescue a sinner like me.

Immanuel's Land. 21

Mrs. Annie Ross Cousin. Wm. J. Kirkpatrick.

1. The sands of time are sinking, The dawn of heav-en breaks; The summer morn I've sighed for—The fair, sweet morn awakes. Dark, dark hath been the midnight, But day-spring is at hand, And glo-ry—glo-ry dwelleth In Immanuel's land, And glory, glory dwelleth In Immanuel's land.

2. O, Christ, he is the fountain, The deep, sweet well of love! The streams on earth I've tasted, More deep I'll drink above: There to an ocean full-ness, His mer-cy doth expand, And glo-ry, glo-ry dwelleth In Immanuel's land, And glory, glory dwelleth In Immanuel's land.

3. I've wrestled on toward heaven, 'Gainst storm and wind and tide, Now like a wea-ry trav-'ler That leaneth on his guide, A-mid the shades of eve-ning, While sinks life's lingering sand, I hail the glo-ry dawning From Immanuel's land, I hail the glory dawning, From Immanuel's land.

4. Deep waters crossed life's pathway, The hedge of thorns was sharp; Now these lie all be-hind me—Oh, for a well tuned harp! Oh, to join the halle-lu-jah With you triumphant band! Who sing where glory dwelleth, In Immanuel's land, Who sing where glory dwelleth, In Immanuel's land.

poco rit.

Copyright, 1891, by Wm. J. Kirkpatrick.

22. When our Ships come Sailing Home.

Rev. Johnson Oatman, Jr.   Jno. R. Sweney.

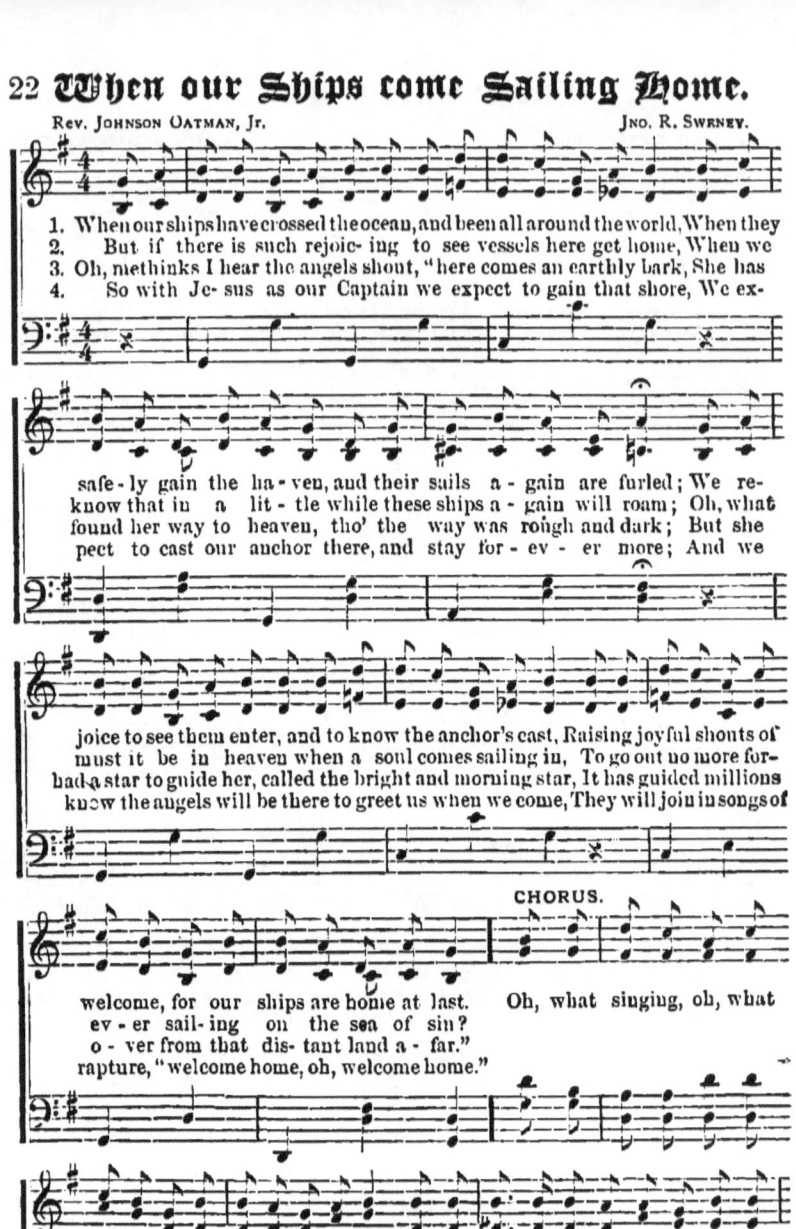

1. When our ships have crossed the ocean, and been all around the world, When they safe-ly gain the ha-ven, and their sails a-gain are furled; We re-joice to see them enter, and to know the anchor's cast, Raising joyful shouts of welcome, for our ships are home at last.
2. But if there is such rejoic-ing to see vessels here get home, When we know that in a lit-tle while these ships a-gain will roam; Oh, what must it be in heaven when a soul comes sailing in, To go out no more for-ev-er sail-ing on the sea of sin?
3. Oh, methinks I hear the angels shout, "here comes an earthly bark, She has found her way to heaven, tho' the way was rough and dark; But she had a star to guide her, called the bright and morning star, It has guided millions o-ver from that dis-tant land a-far."
4. So with Je-sus as our Captain we expect to gain that shore, We ex-pect to cast our anchor there, and stay for-ev-er more; And we know the angels will be there to greet us when we come, They will join in songs of rapture, "welcome home, oh, welcome home."

CHORUS.

Oh, what singing, oh, what shouting, when our ships come sailing home; They have stood the mighty tempests, they have

Copyright, 1894, by Jno R. Sweney.

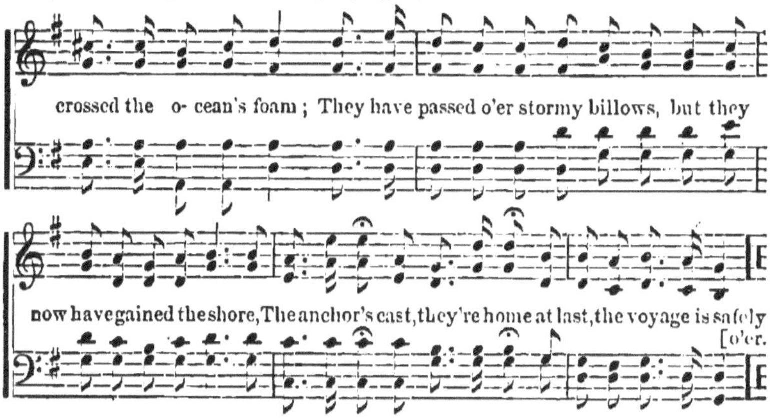

When our Ships, etc.—CONCLUDED.

crossed the o-cean's foam; They have passed o'er stormy billows, but they now have gained the shore, The anchor's cast, they're home at last, the voyage is safely o'er.

Glory to His Name.

Rev. E. A. Hoffman. "I will glorify thy name forevermore." Rev. J. H. Stockton.

1. Down at the cross where my Saviour died, Down where for cleansing from sin I cried; There to my heart was the blood ap-plied; Glo-ry to his name.
2. I am so wondrously saved from sin, Je-sus so sweetly a-bides within; There at the cross where he took me in; Glo-ry to his name.
3. Oh, precious fountain, that saves from sin! I am so glad I have entered in; There Jesus saves me and keeps me clean; Glo-ry to his name.
4. Come to this fountain, so rich and sweet; Cast thy poor soul at the Saviour's feet; Plunge in to-day, and be made complete; Glo-ry to his name.

D.S.—There to my heart was the blood applied; Glo-ry to his name.

Fine. CHORUS. D.S.
name. Glo-ry to his name, Glo-ry to his name;

By permission.

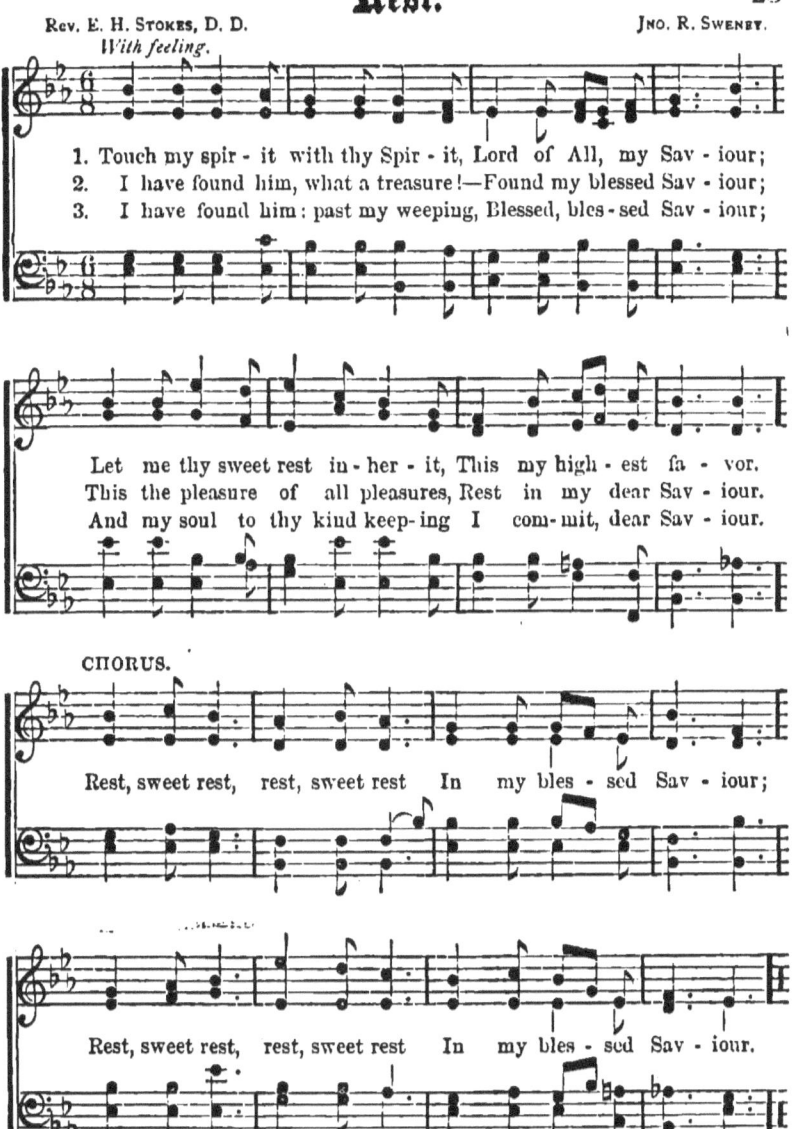

Rest.

Rev. E. H. Stokes, D. D.   Jno. R. Sweney.
With feeling.

1. Touch my spir - it with thy Spir - it, Lord of All, my Sav - iour;
2. I have found him, what a treasure!—Found my blessed Sav - iour;
3. I have found him: past my weeping, Blessed, bles - sed Sav - iour;

Let me thy sweet rest in - her - it, This my high - est fa - vor.
This the pleasure of all pleasures, Rest in my dear Sav - iour.
And my soul to thy kind keep-ing I com - mit, dear Sav - iour.

CHORUS.

Rest, sweet rest, rest, sweet rest In my bles - sed Sav - iour;

Rest, sweet rest, rest, sweet rest In my bles - sed Sav - iour.

4 On the earth this heavenly resting
   Comes to me, dear Saviour;
   This is love's own manifesting,
   Through my blessed Saviour.

5 In this rest toil does not weary,—
   Toil for thee, my Saviour;
   In the gloom there's nothing dreary,
   With thee, O my Saviour.

Copyright, 1885, by John J. Hood.

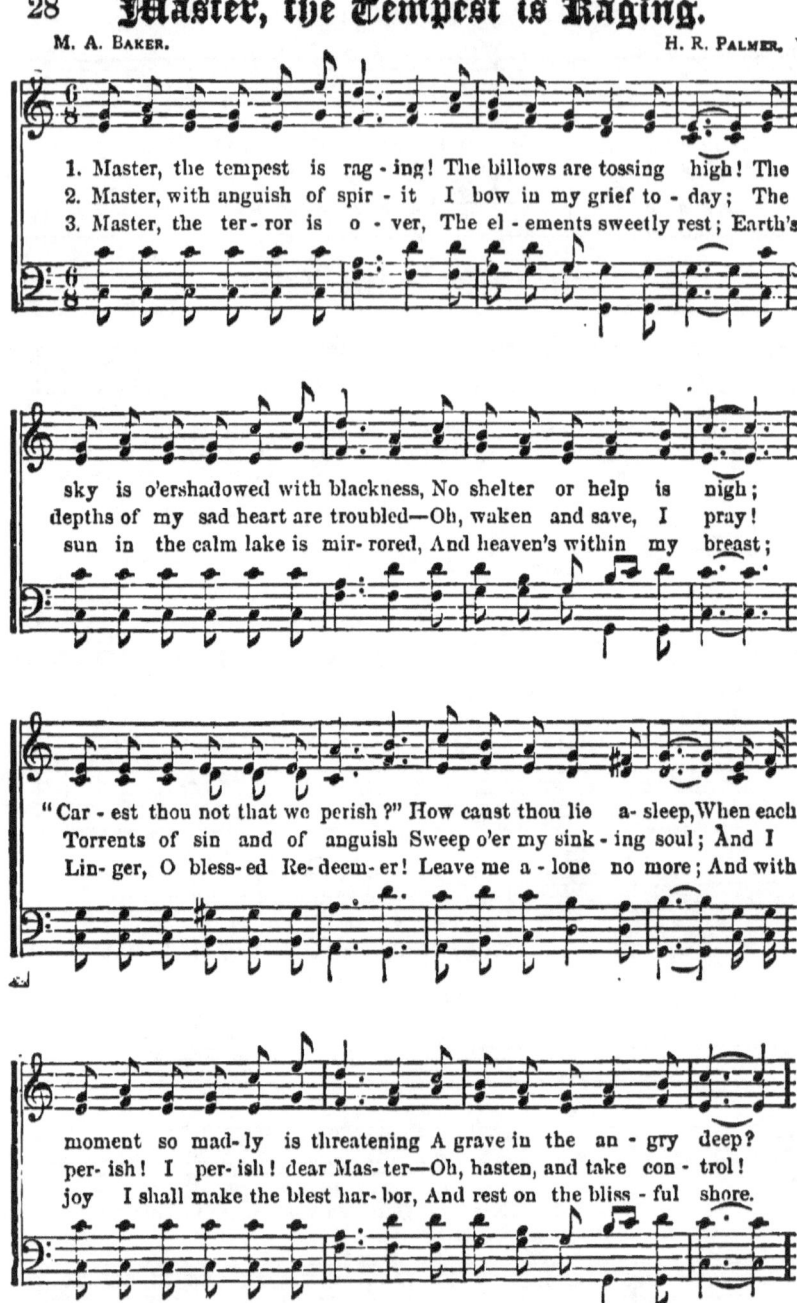

Master, the Tempest, etc.—CONCLUDED.

CHORUS.

The winds and the waves shall obey thy will, Peace, be still! Peace, be still! peace, be still!

Whether the wrath of the storm-tossed sea, Or de-mons or men, or whatever it be, No waters can swallow the ship where lies The Master of ocean, and earth, and skies; They all so sweetly o-bey thy will, Peace, be still!

Peace, be still! They all so sweetly o-bey thy will, Peace, peace, be still!

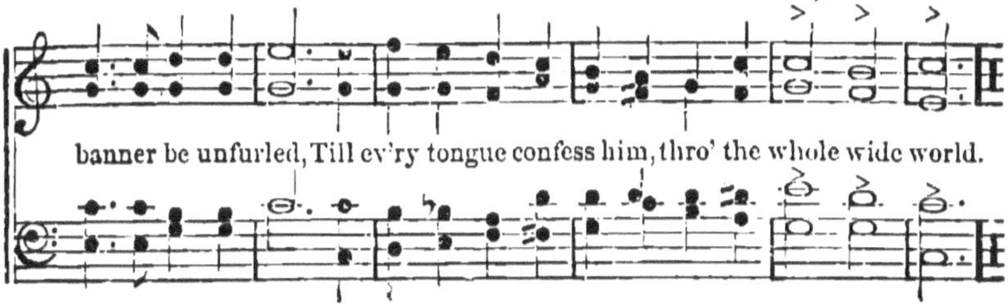

The Whole Wide World.—CONCLUDED. 33

banner be unfurled, Till ev'ry tongue confess him, thro' the whole wide world.

Thou thinkest, Lord, of me.

E. D. MUND.   "The Lord thinketh upon me."—Ps. xl. 17.   E. S. LORENZ.

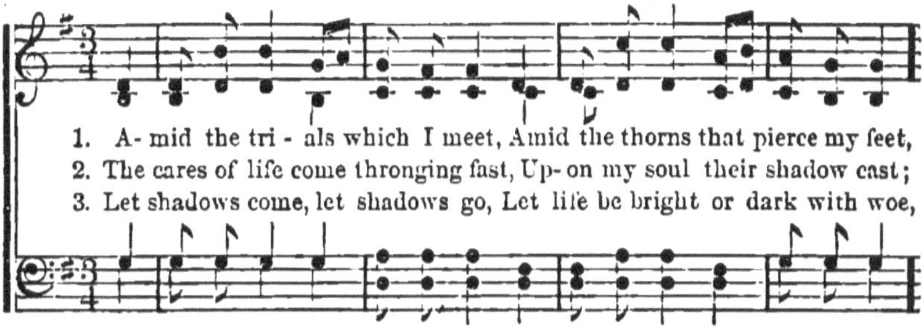

1. A-mid the tri - als which I meet, Amid the thorns that pierce my feet,
2. The cares of life come thronging fast, Up-on my soul their shadow cast;
3. Let shadows come, let shadows go, Let life be bright or dark with woe,

Fine.

One thought remains supreme-ly sweet, Thou thinkest, Lord, of me!
Their gloom reminds my heart at last, Thou thinkest, Lord, of me!
I am con-tent, for this I know, Thou thinkest, Lord, of me!

D. S.—What need I fear since thou art near, And thinkest, Lord, of me.

CHORUS.   D. S.

Thou thinkest, Lord, of me, of me, Thou thinkest, Lord, of me, of me;

By permission.   *Hymn Songs-*C

34 In the Hush of Early Morning.

Mrs. R. N. Turner. Wm. J. Kirkpatrick.

1. In the hush of ear-ly morning, When the breeze is whisp'ring low,
2. When the noontide falls up-on me, With its fer-vid light'ning ray,
3. As the dewy shades steal downward O'er the earth at evening mild,

There's a voice that gent-ly calls me, And its ac-cents well I know!
There's a voice, di-vine-ly earn-est, Bids me work while it is day;
There's a voice I love that whispers, "Af-ter la-bor, rest, my child!"

Here I am, O Saviour, wait-ing; For thy will a-lone is mine,
O-pen, Saviour, now be-fore me All thy will for me to do,
O my Saviour, lov-ing, ten-der, Help me to ac-count it blest

This is all my crown and glo-ry, I am thine, and on-ly thine!
On-ly help me, watching, working, Still to keep my Lord in view!
Thus to work within thy vineyard, Till thou call-est me to rest!

Copyright, 1890, by Wm. J. Kirkpatrick.

Safe within the Vail.

Rev. E. Adams. J. M. Evans.

1. "Land a-head!" its fruits are waving O'er the hills of fadeless green;
2. Onward, bark! the cape I'm rounding; See, the blessed wave their hands,
3. There, let go the anchor, riding On this calm and silv'ry bay;
4. Now we're safe from all temptation, All the storms of life are past;

And the liv-ing waters laving Shores where heav'nly forms are seen.
Hear the harps of God resounding From the bright immor-tal bands.
Seaward fast the tide is gliding, Shores in sunlight stretch away.
Praise the Rock of our Sal-vation, We are safe at home at last.

CHORUS.

Rocks and storms I'll fear no more, When on that e-ter-nal shore,

Drop the an-chor! furl the sail! I am safe within the vail!

36 Abiding.

Rev. E. H. Stokes, D. D.
Jno. R. Sweney.

1. My soul for light and love had earnest longings, Oh, how it longed for fellowship divine! I sought it here and there, I sought it ev'rywhere, At last thro' faith, the ho-ly boon was mine.
2. Oh, how enrich-ing is this sacred treasure! En-riching to this soul, this soul of mine; There's nothing anywhere Can with this love compare, And I henceforth, for-ev-er, Lord, am thine.
3. Oh, yes, I rest, how blessed is the rest-ing! I rest to-day, I'm resting all the time. "Come," echoes thro' the air, "Come," and the resting share, And Je-sus will be yours as he is mine.

CHORUS.

I'm a-bid-ing, gracious Sa-viour, I'm a-bid-ing in thy precious love to-day; I'm a-bid-ing, yes, a-bid-ing In thy love, thy precious love, to-day.

Copyright 1882, by John J. Hood.

Good News.—CONCLUDED.

D.C. Chorus.

mer - cy. Re - deemed thro' the Son of his love.
         we're redeemed   the Son of his love.
turn - ing, The home, and the glad welcome there.
      heav'nly home,   the glad welcome there.
Sav - iour, He died, and is ris - en a - gain.
      died for us,   is ris-en again.

My Jesus, as Thou wilt.

BENJAMIN SCHMOLKA. Tr. by Miss J. BORTHWICK.   Tune, JEWETT. 6s.

1. My Je - sus, as thou wilt: O may thy will be mine; In - to thy
2. My Je - sus, as thou wilt: Tho' seen thro' many-a tear, Let not my
3. My Je - sus, as thou wilt: All shall be well for me; Each changing

band of love I would my all re - sign. Thro' sor - row or thro' joy,
star of hope Grow dim or dis - ap - pear. Since thou on earth hast wept
fu - ture scene I glad - ly trust with thee. Straight to my home a - bove,

Conduct me as thine own, And help me still to say, "My Lord, thy will be done."
And sorrowed oft alone, If I must weep with thee, My Lord, thy will be done.
I trav - el calmly on, And sing in life or death, "My Lord, thy will be done."

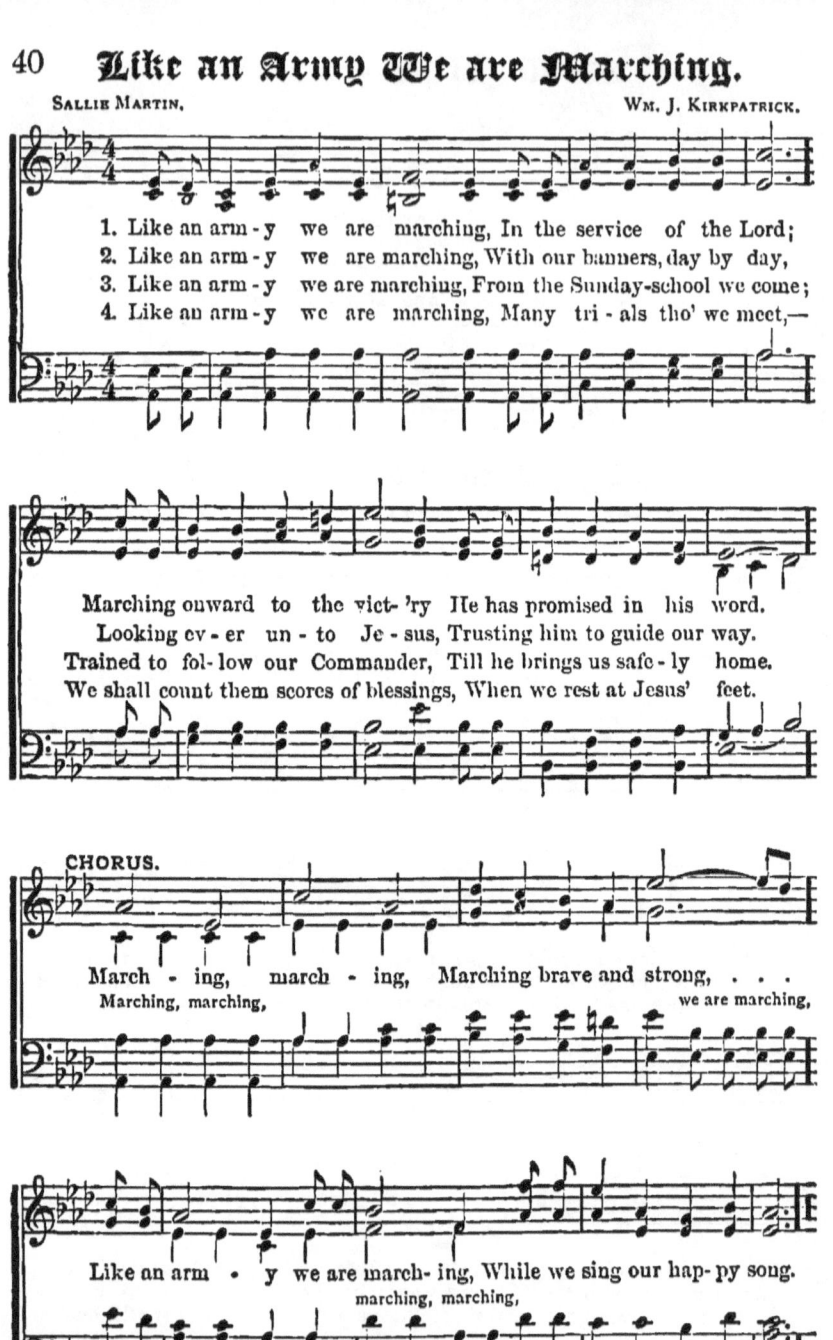

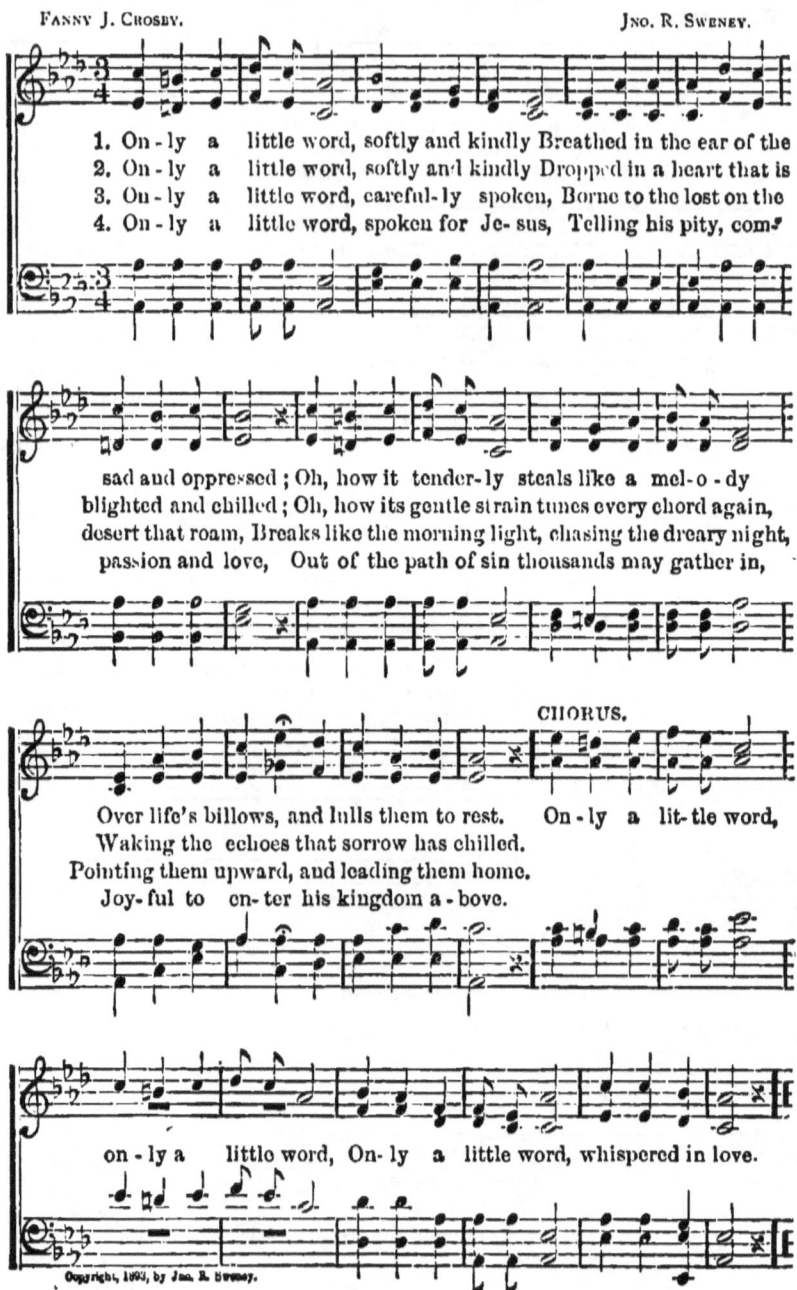

Marching on to Canaan.

"They shall march with an army."—Jer. xlvi: 22.

Rev. M. Lowrie Hofford.   W. A. Ogden. By per.

1. We are marching on to Canaan, And Jehovah is our guide;
2. We are marching thro' the desert, And the manna all around
3. We are marching thro' the desert To the promised land divine,

We are marching thro' the desert, He is ever at our side;
And the dew of night is falling, And is cov'ring all the ground;
To the land of milk and honey, To the land of corn and wine;

DUET.

In the darkness or the danger We can never go astray,
From the smitten rock the waters, In their sparkling fulness flow,
We are marching thro' the desert, And we near the shining shore,

With Jehovah for our leader And our guide upon the way.
Thus delighting and refreshing All the weary journey through.
From our home beyond the Jordan We shall wander never more.

FULL CHORUS.

On, steadily on! Steadily marching to the happy land of
Marching on, marching on, we're

Copyright, 1885, by W. A. Ogden.

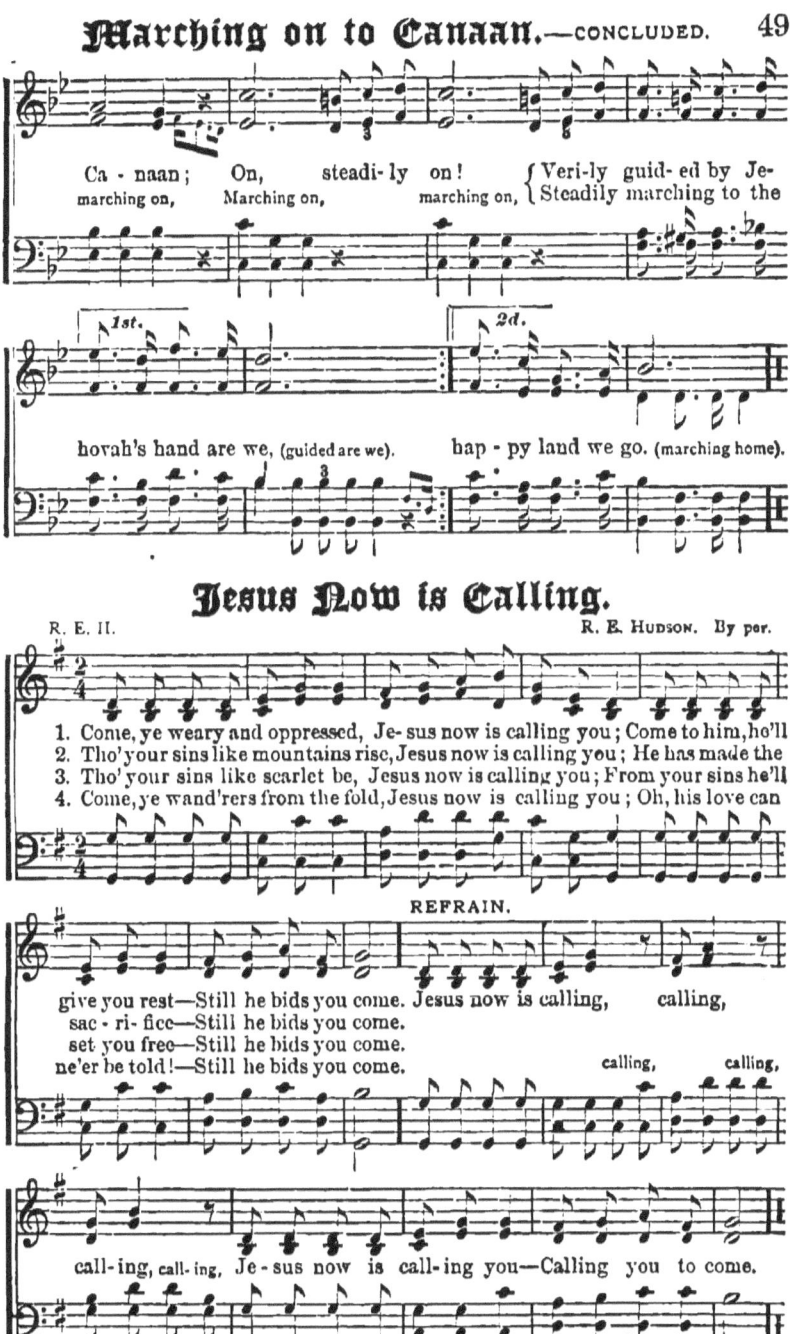

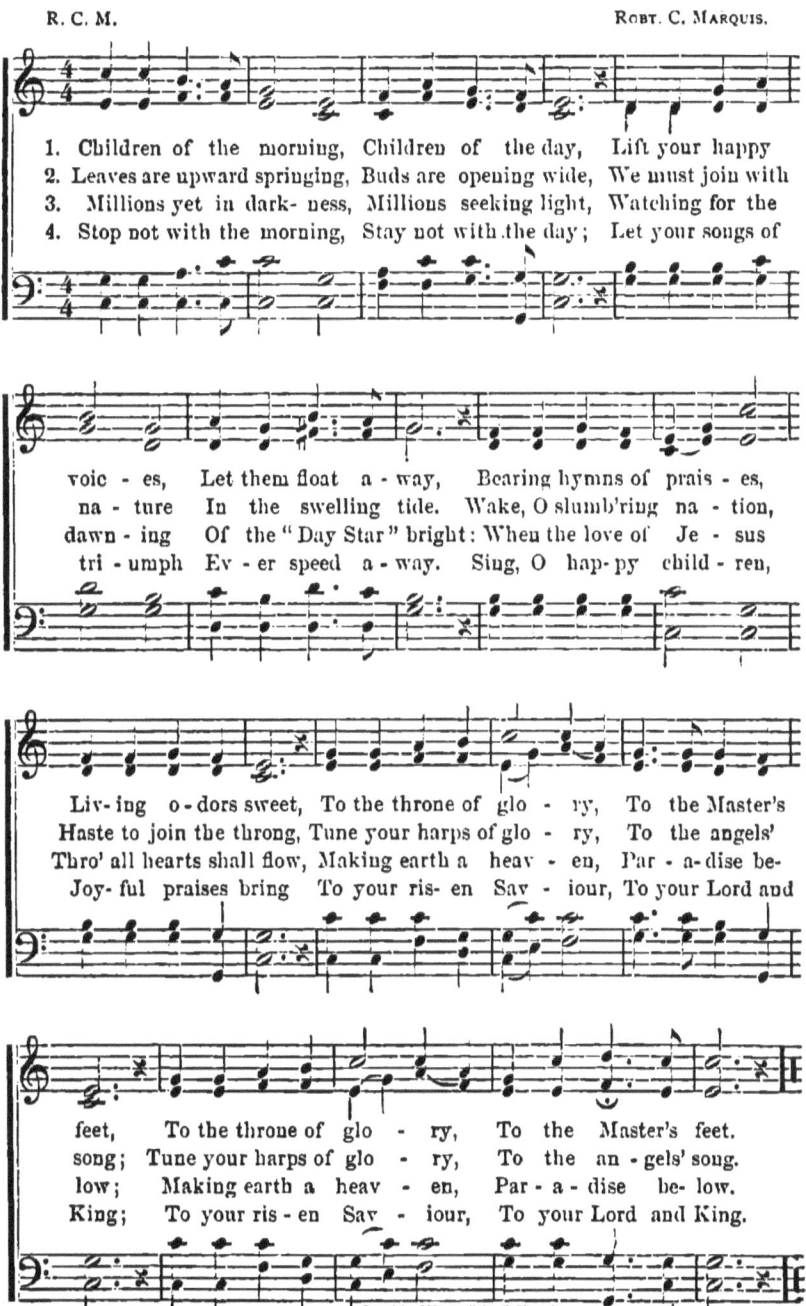

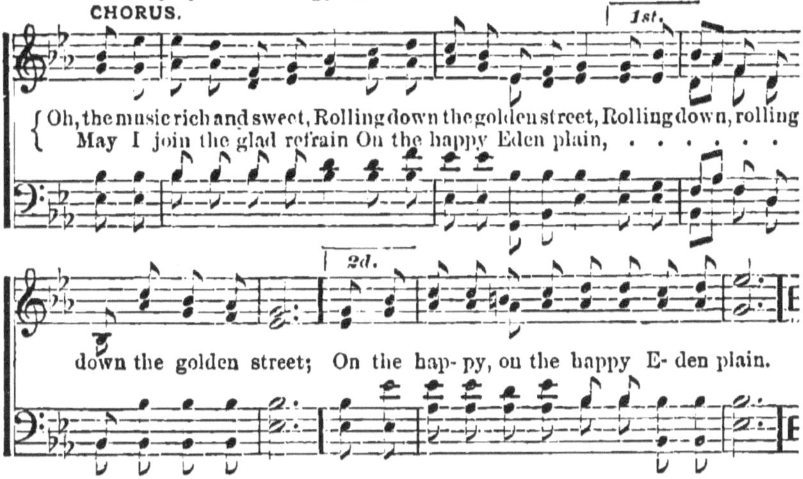

Heavenly Music.—CONCLUDED.

CHORUS.

Oh, the music rich and sweet, Rolling down the golden street, Rolling down, rolling down the golden street; On the hap-py, on the happy E-den plain.

May I join the glad refrain On the happy Eden plain, ...

The Fountain Now is Open Wide.

COWPER. WM. J. KIRKPATRICK.

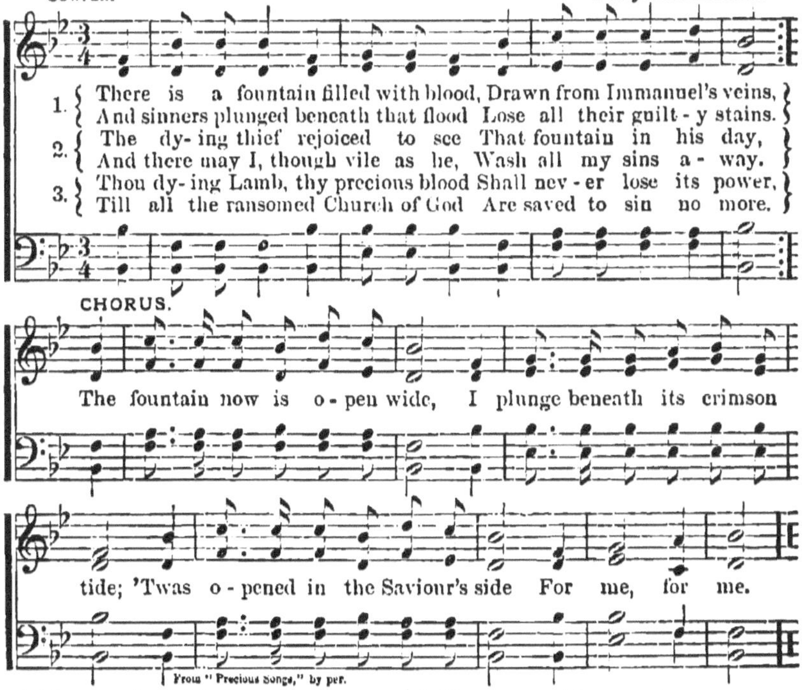

1. There is a fountain filled with blood, Drawn from Immanuel's veins,
   And sinners plunged beneath that flood Lose all their guilt-y stains.
2. The dy-ing thief rejoiced to see That fountain in his day,
   And there may I, though vile as he, Wash all my sins a-way.
3. Thou dy-ing Lamb, thy precious blood Shall nev-er lose its power,
   Till all the ransomed Church of God Are saved to sin no more.

CHORUS.

The fountain now is o-pen wide, I plunge beneath its crimson tide; 'Twas o-pened in the Saviour's side For me, for me.

From "Precious Songs," by per.

4 E'er since by faith I saw the stream
  Thy flowing wounds supply,
  Redeeming love has been my theme,
  And shall be till I die.

5 Then in a nobler, sweeter song
  I'll sing thy power to save,
  When this poor lisping, stamm'ring
  Lies silent in the grave. [tongue

Harvest Time.

W. A. S.   W. A. Spencer.

1. The seed I have scattered in spring-time with weeping, And watered with tears and with dews from on high;
 An-oth-er may shout when the harvesters reaping Shall gath-er my grain in the "sweet by and by."

CHORUS.
O-ver and o-ver, yes, deep-er and deep-er My heart is pierced through with life's sorrow-ing cry, But the
By and by, by and by, By and by, by and by, Yes, the

D. S.— tears of the sow-er and songs of the reap-er Shall min-gle to-gether in joy by and by.

Copyright, 1886, by John J. Hood.

2 Another may reap what in spring-time I've planted,
   Another rejoice in the fruit of my pain,—
   Not knowing my tears when in summer I fainted
   While toiling sad-hearted in sunshine and rain.

3 The thorns will have choked, and the summer sun blasted
   The most of the seed which in spring-time I've sown;
   But the Lord who has watched while my weary toil lasted
   Will give me a harvest for what I have done.

The Morning Draweth Nigh. 65

FANNY J. CROSBY.   JNO. R. SWENEY.

1. Oh, ral - ly round the stand-ard Of Christ, our roy - al King; Oh,
2. Tho' long and deep the sha - dows The dreary night may bring, Our
3. To yon-der gold - en reg - ion Our faith now plumes her wing; Our
4. To him who paid our ran - som, And took from death the sting. Be

CHORUS.

ral - ly round his stand-ard, And hal - le - lu - jahs sing. For the
lamps are trimm'd and burn-ing, Our hal - le - lu - jahs ring.
hearts with joy are bound-ing, And hal - le - lu - jahs ring.
ev - er - last-ing prais - es, Let hal - le - lu - jahs ring.

morn - - - ing draweth nigh,   For the morn - - -
morning draweth nigh,   For the morning draweth nigh, Hal - le - lu - jah! hal - le -

- - - ing draweth nigh;   We can see . . . it in the
lu - jah! yes, the morn-ing draw-eth nigh;   We can see it, we can

dis - tance,   We shall hear it, we shall hear it by and by. by and by.
see it in the distance,

Copyright, 1890, by Jno. R. Sweney.

We are Building on the Rock. 67

JENNIE WILSON. Luke vi: 48. I. H. MEREDITH.

1. We are building on the Rock, the Rock of A-ges, Tow'ring grandly o-ver
2. We are building on the Rock, the Rock of A-ges, Safe tho' angry billows
3. We are building on the safe and sure foundation, God in loving mercy
4. We are building for the coming years e-ternal, When like fitful dreams shall

times tempestuous sea; We are building on the Rock, the Rock of Ages, Safely
fiercely 'round us beat; There abiding while the tempest wildly rages, Harm can
for our souls has laid; There alone is found the fortress of salvation, There a-
earthly things be past; Building firmly for the future life super-nal On the

REFRAIN.

building for e-ter-ni-ty.   We are build-ing
nev-er reach this calm re-treat.
lone may ev-'ry hope be staid.
Rock that shall for-ev-er last.   building on the Rock,

build-ing. We are building on the Rock of A-ges, We are build-ing,
building on the Rock,   building on the Rock,

build-ing, We are building for e-ter-ni-ty.
building on the Rock,

Copyright, 1894, by John J. Hood.

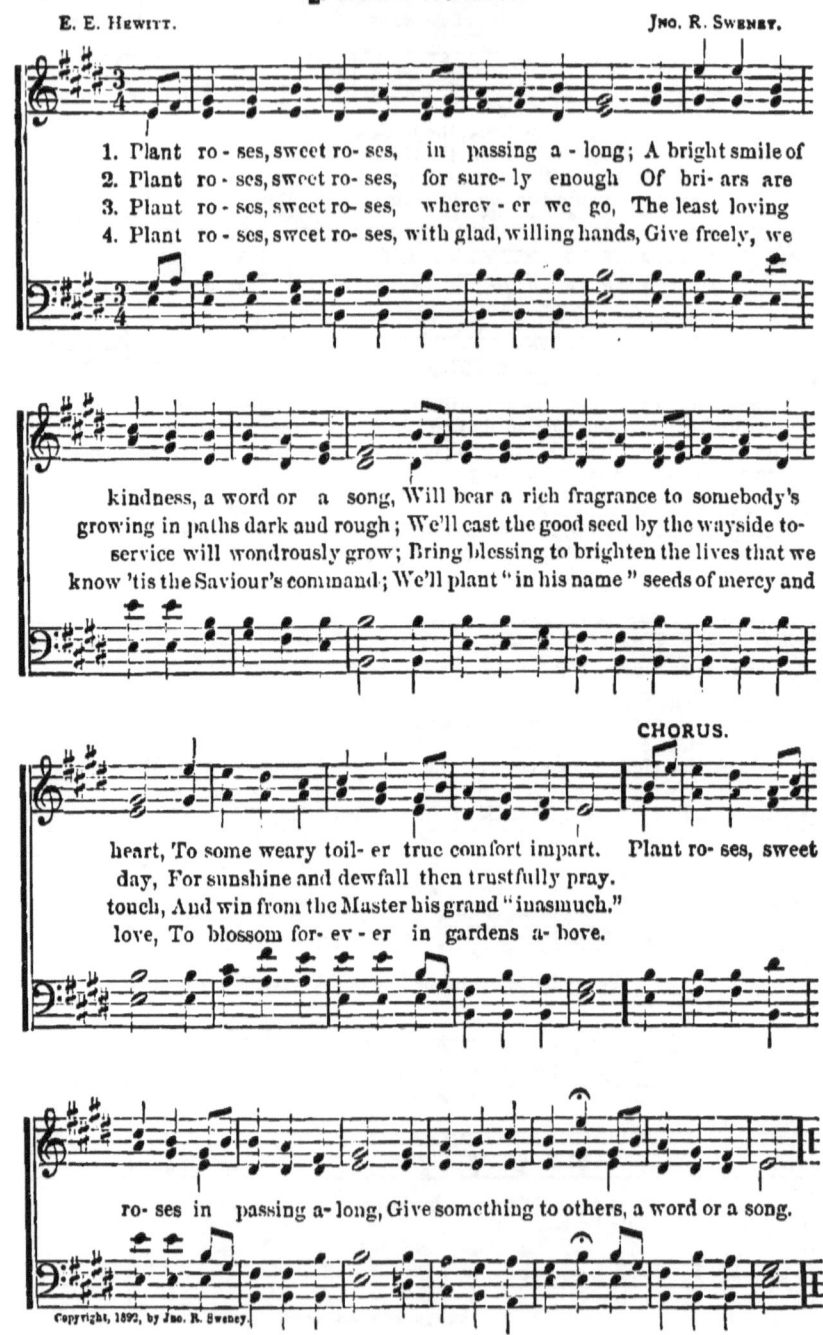

70. Behold Me Standing at the Door!

"Behold, I stand at the door, and knock."—Rev. iii: 20.

FANNY J. CROSBY.   Mrs. JOS. F. KNAPP. By per.

1. Be-hold Me standing at the door, And hear Me pleading ev-er-more, With gentle voice, oh, heart of sin, May I come in? may I come in?
2. I bore the cruel thorns for thee; I wait-ed long and patient-ly: Say, wea-ry heart, oppress'd with sin, May I come in? may I come in?
3. I would not plead with thee in vain; Re-member all My grief and pain! I died to ran-som thee from sin, May I come in? may I come in?
4. I bring thee joy from heav'n above; I bring thee pardon, peace and love: Say, wea-ry heart, oppress'd with sin, May I come in? may I come in?

CHORUS.

Be-hold Me standing at the door, And hear Me pleading ev-er-more: Say, wea-ry heart, oppress'd with sin, May I come in? may I come in?

Sing On.—CONCLUDED.

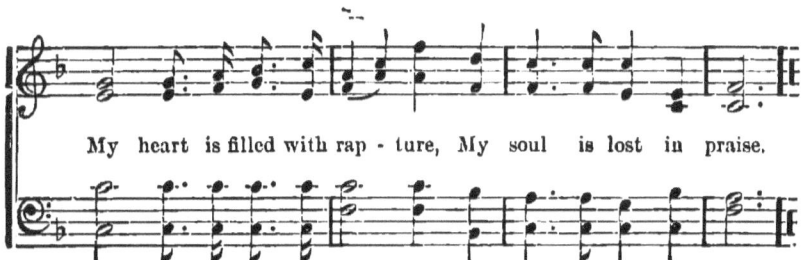

We are Nearing.

FANNY J. CROSBY.   JNO. R. SWENEY.

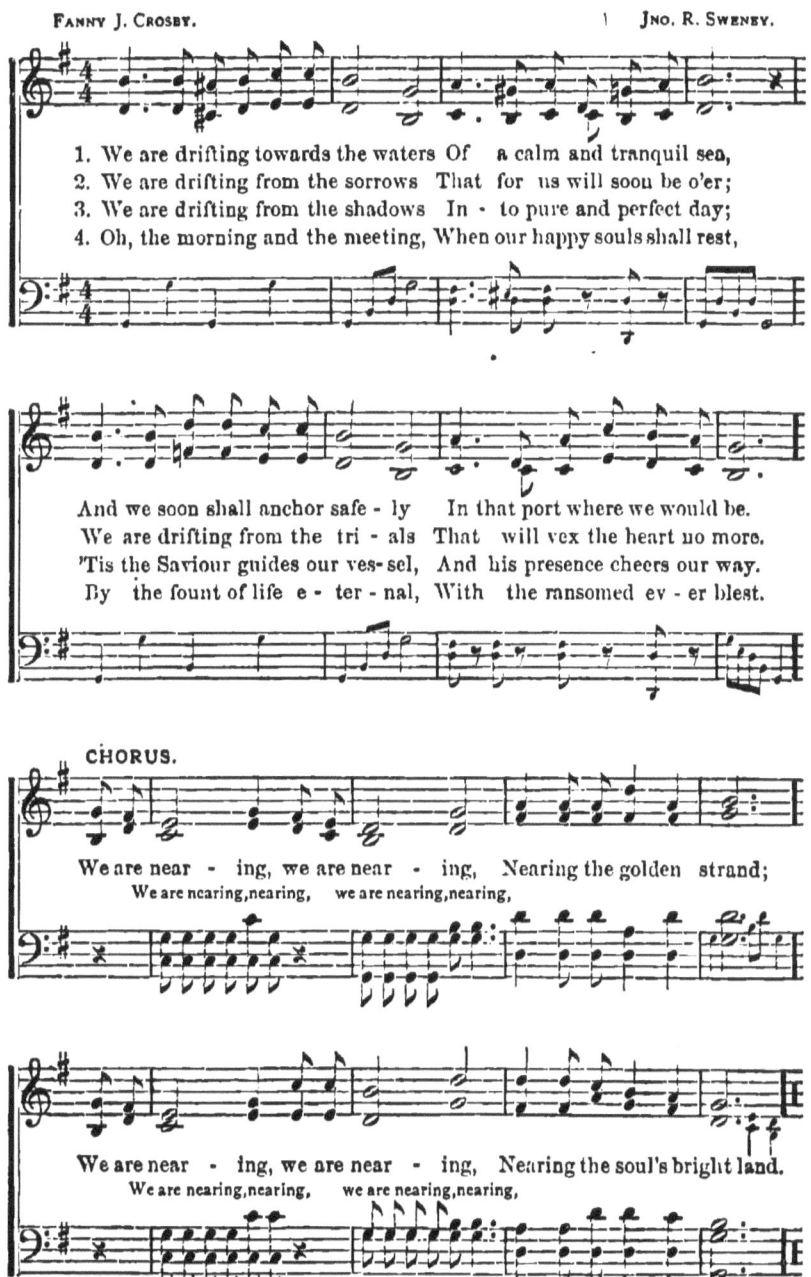

1. We are drifting towards the waters Of a calm and tranquil sea,
2. We are drifting from the sorrows That for us will soon be o'er;
3. We are drifting from the shadows In-to pure and perfect day;
4. Oh, the morning and the meeting, When our happy souls shall rest,

And we soon shall anchor safe-ly In that port where we would be.
We are drifting from the tri-als That will vex the heart no more.
'Tis the Saviour guides our ves-sel, And his presence cheers our way.
By the fount of life e-ter-nal, With the ransomed ev-er blest.

CHORUS.

We are near-ing, we are near-ing, Nearing the golden strand;
We are nearing, nearing, we are nearing, nearing,

We are near-ing, we are near-ing, Nearing the soul's bright land.
We are nearing, nearing, we are nearing, nearing,

Copyright, 1892, by Jno R. Sweney.

Hymn Songs-F

Only a Beam of Sunshine.—CONCLUDED. 85

O - ver some grief-worn spir - it May rest like a sunbeam fair.

"Mizpah."

"Mizpah; . . The Lord watch between me and thee, when we are absent one from another."
Gen. xxxi. 49.

E. E. HEWITT.   WM. J. KIRKPATRICK.

1. Let us ask the precious Sav - iour To go with us while we part.
2. Know we not what changes wait us, But we know our mighty Guide,
3. In his tender hands entrust - ing Ev - 'ry link in love's bright chain;
4. Meet a - gain, no more to sev - er, In the "beautiful beyond,"

For his presence in life's journey Peace and comfort will impart.
Safe are we in his dear keeping, Hap - py, when he walks beside.
'Tis a blessed hope that whispers, Sure - ly we shall meet a - gain.
Where the love of our Redeem - er Is the strongest, sweetest bond.

CHORUS.

Long our hallowed prayer will lin - ger, Mingling with sweet melo - dy;

Poco ritard.

Be our wish at parting, "Mizpah," May the Lord keep watch over you and me.

Copyright, 1890, by Wm. J. Kirkpatrick.

86. Wonderful Story of Love.

M. Taylor.   Rev. Arthur J. Smith.

1. To-day God is tell-ing a won-derful sto-ry, The tru-est, the grandest that ev-er was told; The fullest disclosure of grace and of glo-ry, Kept hidden from all the prophets of old.
2. He brings the as-sur-ance of present sal-va-tion, E-ter-nal as God's own immu-ta-ble throne, Deliv'rance forever from all condem-na-tion, A standing in Christ, the place of a son.
3. This, then, is the day when with love far ex-ceeding, With all that he has, God would lost ones endow, The acceptable time, e'en the time of his pleading, The day of salvation, God's wonder-ful NOW.

CHORUS.

To-day we're tell-ing the sto-ry, Won-derful, won-derful sto-ry, To-day we're telling the story, The wonderful story of love.

Copyright, 1890, property of John J. Hood.

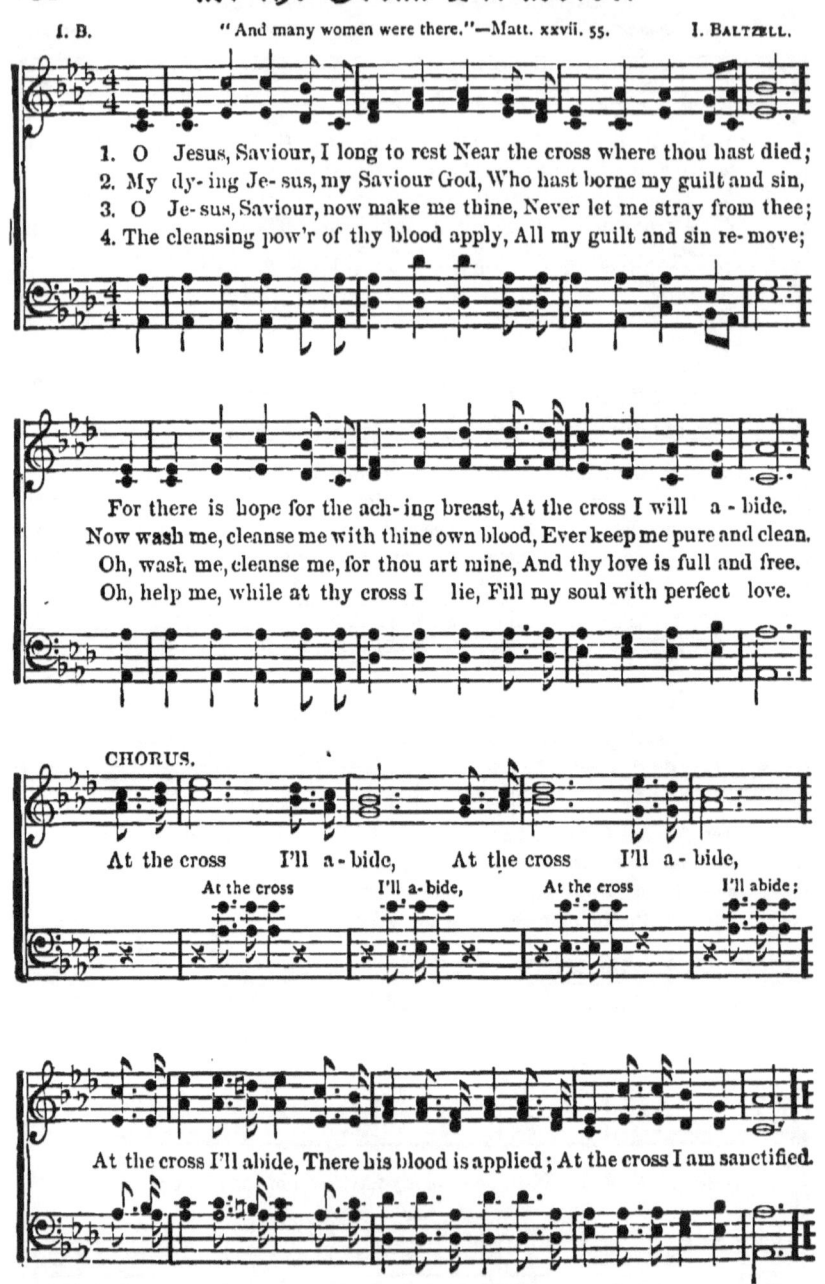

I Will Go.

89

MARTHA J. LANKTON.   WM. J. KIRKPATRICK.

1. I will go, I can-not stay From the arms of love a-way;
2. Though I long have tried in vain, Tried to break the tempter's chain,
3. I am lost, and yet I know Earth can nev-er heal my woe;
4. Something whispers in my soul, Though my sins like mountains roll,
5. I o-bey the Saviour's call, Now to him I yield my all,

Oh, for strength of faith to say, Je - sus died for me.
Yet to-night I'll try a - gain, Je - sus, help thou me.
I will rise at once and go, Je - sus died for me.
Je - sus' blood will make me whole, Je - sus died for me.
At his feet, where oth - ers fall, There's a place for me.

CHORUS.

Can it be, oh, can it be There is hope for one like me?

rit.

I will go with this my plea, Je - sus died for me.

Copyright, 1888, by WM. J. KIRKPATRICK.

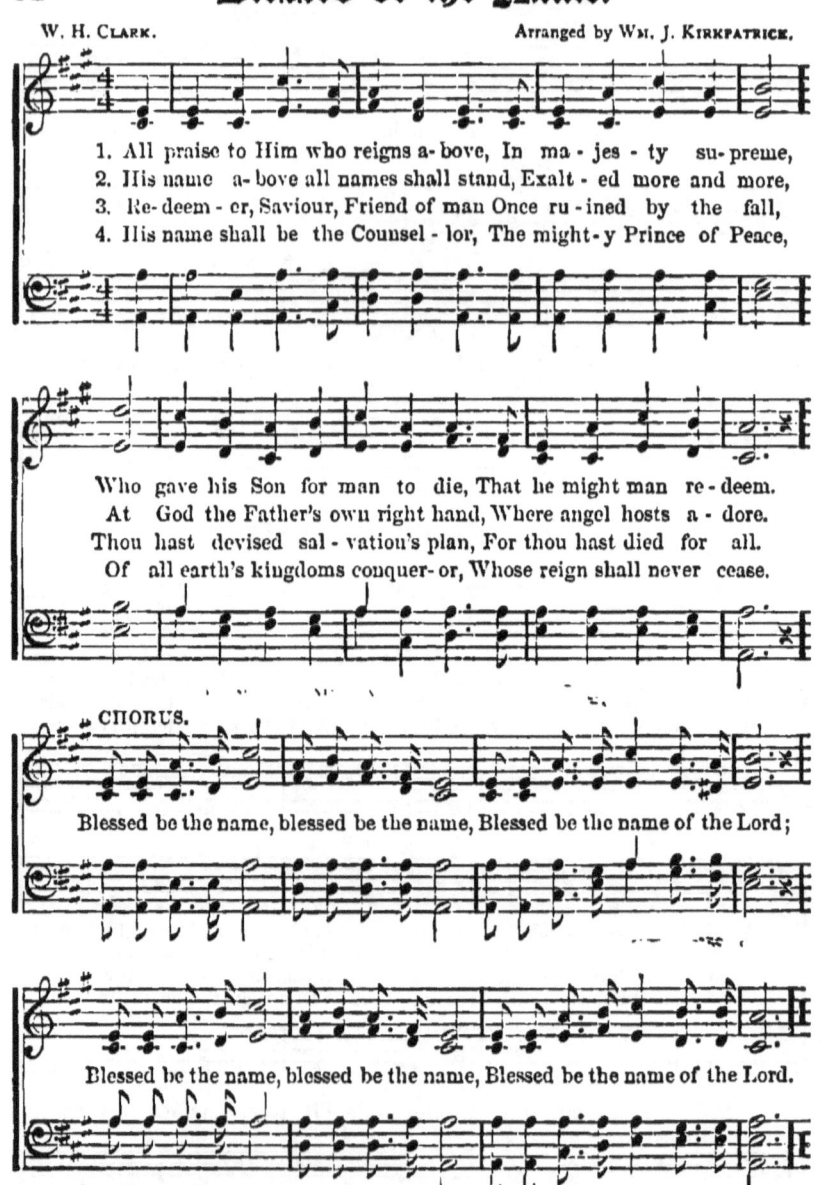

4 Walk the waves, across life's sea,
  Jesus, the light of the world;
 Nearer come, O Lord, to me,
  Jesus, the light of the world.

5 Be a shelter in the storm,
  Jesus, the light of the world;
 Keep, oh, keep thy child from harm,
  Jesus, the light of the world.

Pleading with Thee.

95

J. JACKSON   WM. J. KIRKPATRICK.

1. Wea-ry, oh, yes, thou art wea-ry, Bearing thy burden of sin;
2. Lone-ly, oh, yes, thou art lone-ly, Plodding thy desolate way,
3. Troubled, oh, yes, thou art troubled; Comfort has flown from thy breast;
4. Wea-ry and lonely and trou-bled, Broken in spir-it and heart,

Clouds of the night are above thee, Fear and temptation with-in.
Far from the arms that would shield thee, Far from the light and the day.
On-ly in Je-sus thy re-fuge, On-ly in him is thy rest.
Come to thy gracious Redeem-er: Child of his mer-cy thou art.

CHORUS.

Hear the sweet voice that is pleading with thee,
          Pleading with thee, pleading with thee,
Hear the sweet voice that is pleading with thee, Tenderly pleading with thee,
          Plead - - - - ing with thee.

Copyright, 1886, by WM. J. KIRKPATRICK.

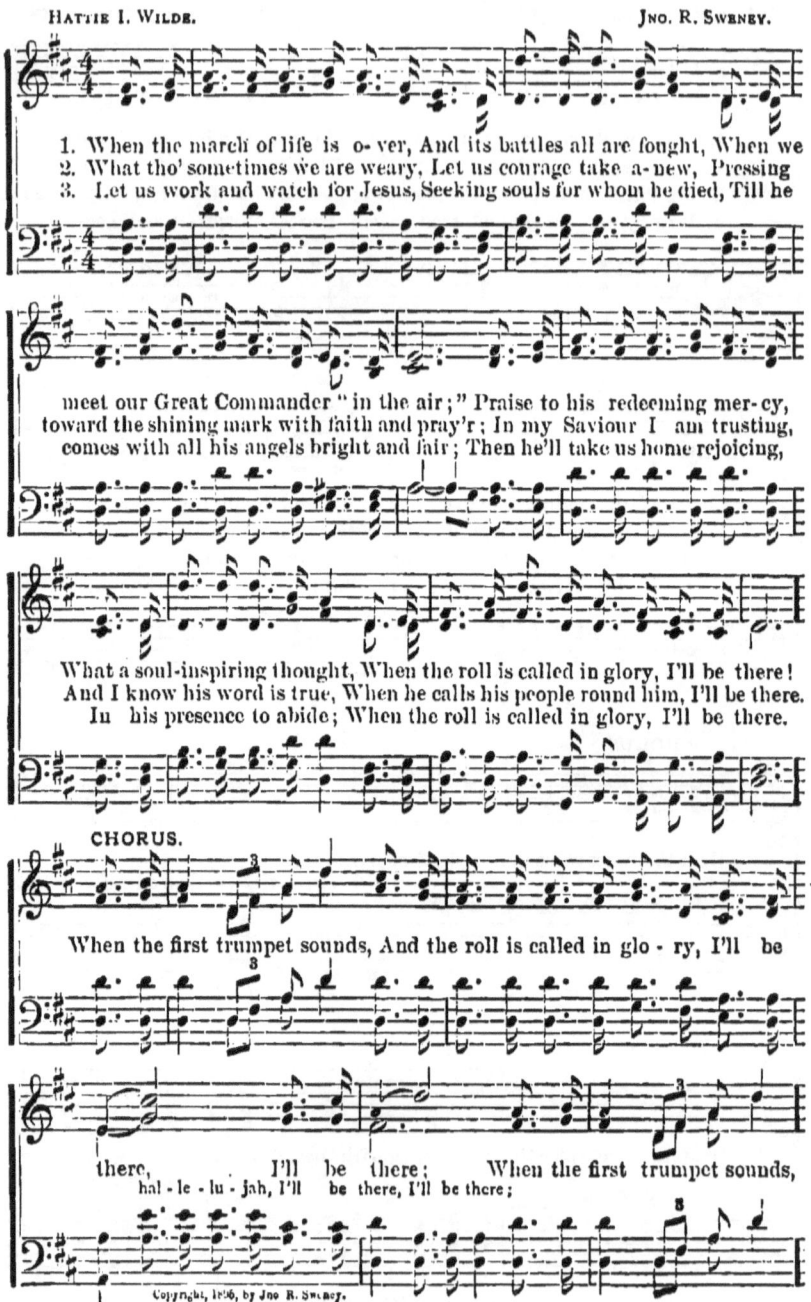

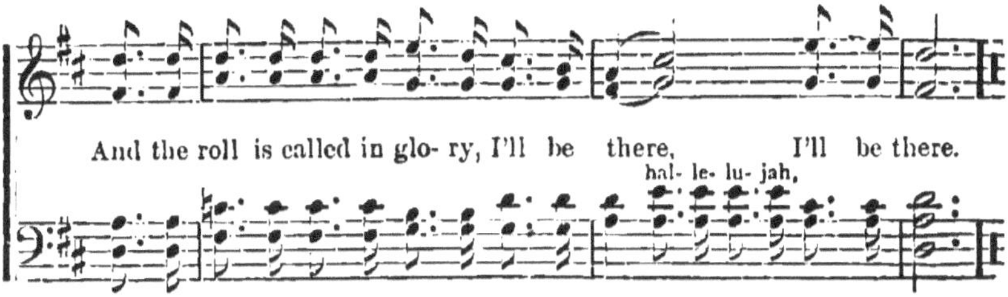

The Roll Call.—CONCLUDED.   97

And the roll is called in glo-ry, I'll be there, (hal-le-lu-jah,) I'll be there.

Have a Little Talk with Jesus.

Rev. JOHNSON OATMAN, Jr.   To Mr. Jas. N. Clemmer.   JNO. R. SWENEY.

1. When dark and dreary is my road, When faint and weary with my load ; 'Tis
2. I tell him all a-bout my care, He helps me ev'ry burden bear; I
3. How dark and drear this world would be, Had we no guide across life's sea ; In
4. Where could we look for guiding light, Did we not have this day-star bright? This

Fine.

then I seek his blest a-bode, And have a lit-tle talk with Je - sus.
al-ways find a blessing there, When I have a lit-tle talk with Je - sus.
time of storm no place to flee, And have a lit-tle talk with Je - sus.
world would be a cheerless night, Without a lit-tle talk with Je - sus.

D. S.—faith we meet him face to face, And have a lit-tle talk with Je - sus.

CHORUS.   D.S.

O praise him for his wondrous grace, In ev-'ry tri-al, in ev'ry place ; By

Copyright, 1895, by Jno. R. Sweney.

5 In times of peace, in times of strife,
   Let joy prevail, or fears be rife ;
   I'll always seek this friend thro' life,
   And have a little talk wi ✝ Jesus.

6 And after life with me is o'er,
   I'll enter in thro' mercy's door,
   And with the millions gone before,
   I'll ever live and talk with Jesus.

Hymn Songs-G

I will Shout His Praise.—CONCLUDED. 99

glo - ry, . . . So will I, so will I, And we'll all sing hallelujah in heaven by and by.

Hold On, My Soul.

WM. H. JONES.
JNO. R. SWENEY.

1. Hold on, my soul, to the end hold out, With a faith no storm can shock;
2. Hold on, my soul, tho' the lightenings flash, And thy sails all torn may be,
3. Hold on, my soul, tho' the waves run high, For the night and storm shall cease,
4. Hold on, my soul, for the end draws near, And thy voyage is well nigh o'er,

Fine.

Stand firm, stand fast, for the Lord has said He will hide thee in the rifted rock.
For thy hope still points to the polar star, Brightly shining thro' the clouds for thee.
There is light beyond, 'tis the morning breaks, Thou art coming to the port of peace.
And the welcome-home thou hast longed to hear Soon will greet thee on the golden shore.

D.S.—on, my soul, for the Lord has said He will hide thee in the rifted rock.

CHORUS. *D.S.*

Hold on, (hold on,) hold on, (hold on,) With a faith no storm can shock, Hold

Copyright, 1890, by Jno. R. Sweney.

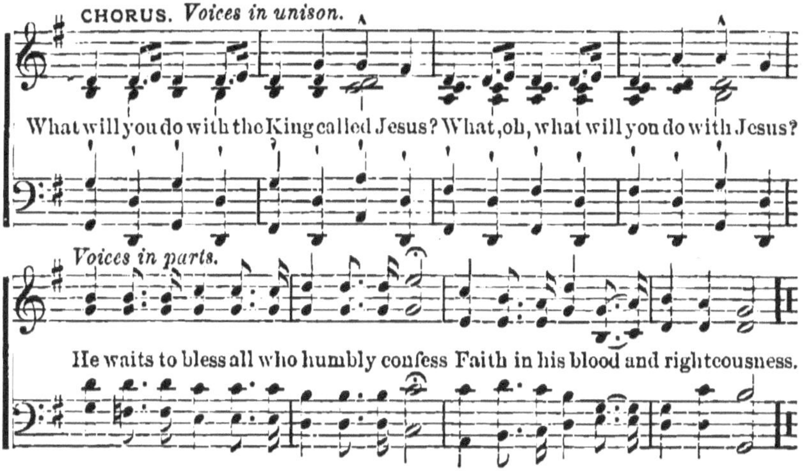

What will You do?—CONCLUDED. 105

CHORUS. *Voices in unison.*

What will you do with the King called Jesus? What, oh, what will you do with Jesus?

Voices in parts.

He waits to bless all who humbly confess Faith in his blood and righteousness.

Consecration.

Mrs. Mary D. James. Mrs. Jos. F. Knapp.

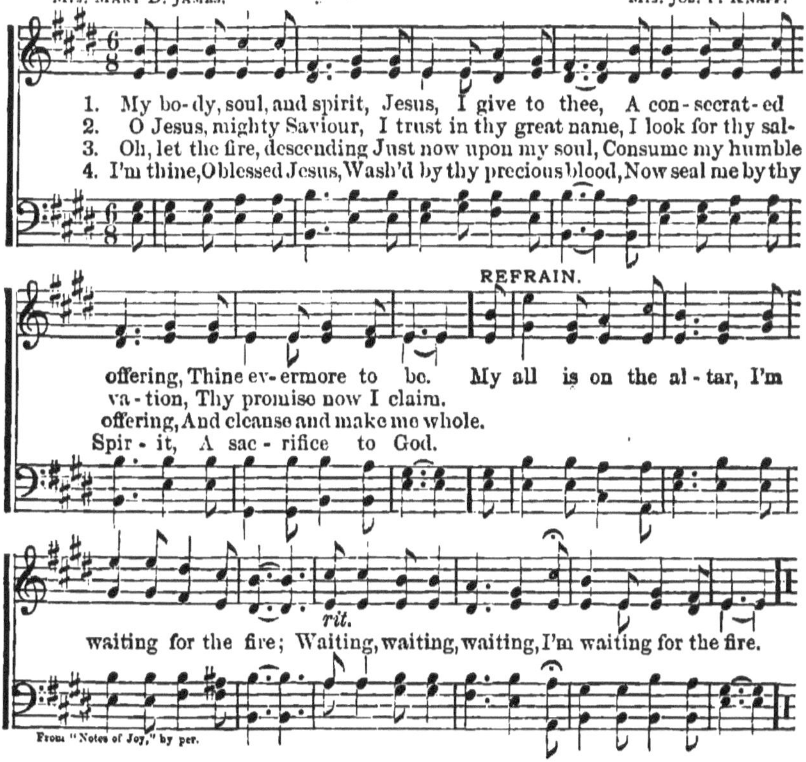

1. My bo-dy, soul, and spirit, Jesus, I give to thee, A con-secrat-ed
2. O Jesus, mighty Saviour, I trust in thy great name, I look for thy sal-
3. Oh, let the fire, descending Just now upon my soul, Consume my humble
4. I'm thine, O blessed Jesus, Wash'd by thy precious blood, Now seal me by thy

REFRAIN.

offering, Thine ev-ermore to be. My all is on the al-tar, I'm
va-tion, Thy promise now I claim.
offering, And cleanse and make me whole.
Spir-it, A sac-rifice to God.

rit.

waiting for the fire; Waiting, waiting, waiting, I'm waiting for the fire.

From "Notes of Joy," by per.

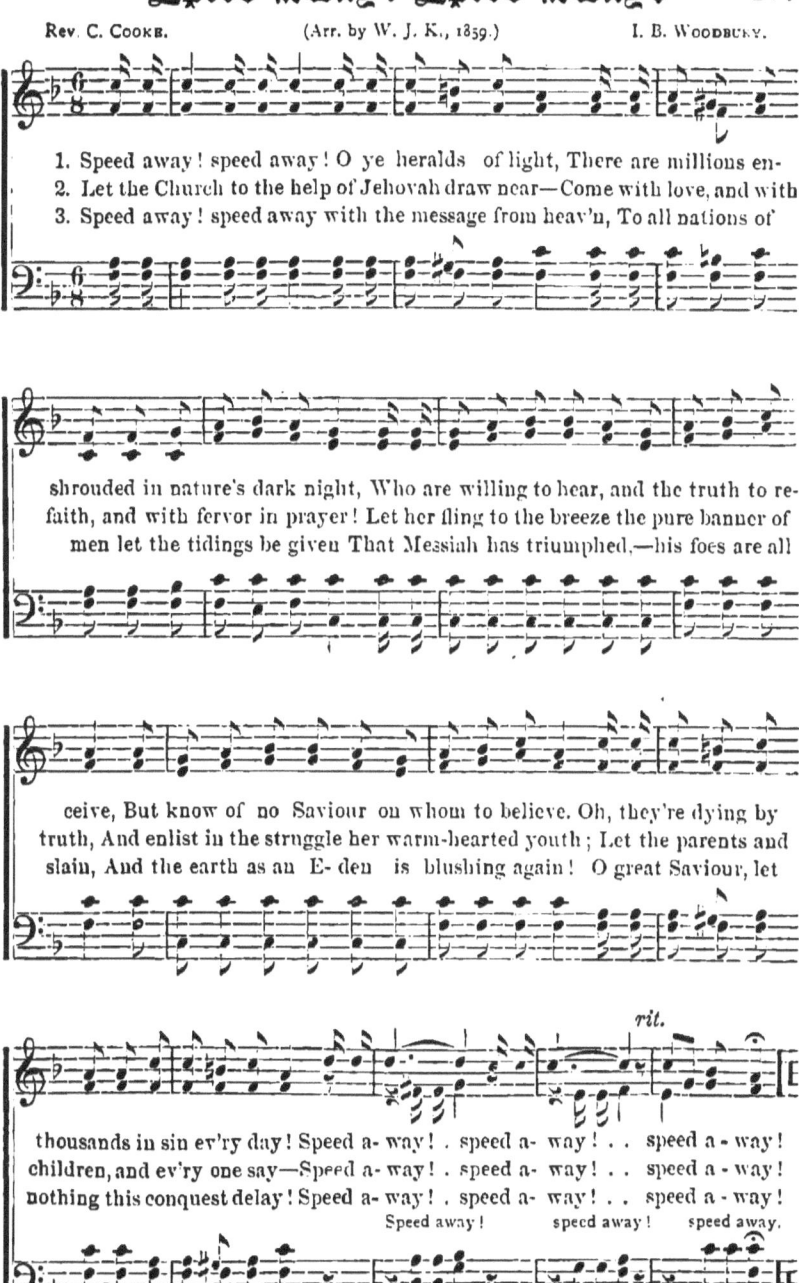

The Endeavor Band.—CONCLUDED.

Our Sunday School. *Music above.*

1 Our Sunday-school, how sweet, how dear
To meet and learn of Jesus here;
To read his word, whose ev'ry line
Is full of hope and joy divine.

CHO.—Our blessed Sunday-school,
Our bright and happy home,
Within thy peaceful dome
We love, we love to come;
Our thoughts will cling to thee,
And still our prayer will be,
That God may bless and keep our
Sunday-school.

2 Our Sunday school, where all may sing
Glad songs of praise to God our King,
And youthful hearts may find the way
To perfect peace and endless day.

3 Our school is like a garden fair,
Where plants are trained with tender care
To bloom for him, the Lord of all,
Whose loving smiles like sunbeams fall.

4 Our Sunday-school, whose golden hours
From Eden bring refreshing showers,
In thee on earth we learn to live,
For thee our thanks to God we give.

All for Jesus.

MARY D. JAMES.   Arranged.

3 Since my eyes were fixed on Jesus,
I've lost sight of all besides;
So enchained my spirit's vision,
Looking at the Crucified.
‖: All for Jesus! all for Jesus!
Looking at the Crucified. :‖

4 Oh, what wonder! how amazing!
Jesus, glorious King of kings—
Deigns to call me his beloved,
Lets me rest beneath his wings.
‖: All for Jesus! all for Jesus!
Resting now beneath his wings! :‖

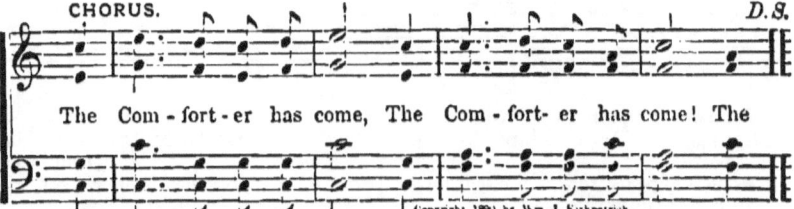

Wonderful Love of Jesus. 113

"The love of Christ, which passeth knowledge."
Eph. iii. 19.

E. D. MUND.   E. S. LORENZ.

1. In vain in high and ho-ly lays My soul her grateful voice would raise; For who can sing the worthy praise Of the won-derful love of Je-sus?
2. A joy by day, a peace by night, In storms a calm, in darkness light; In pain a balm, in weakness might, Is the won-derful love of Je-sus.
3. My hope for pardon when I call, My trust for lift-ing when I fall; In life, in death, my all in all, Is the won-derful love of Je-sus.

CHORUS.

Won-derful love! won-derful love! Won-der-ful love of Je-sus!

Wonder-ful love! won-derful love! Wonder-ful love of Je-sus!

From "Holy Voices," by per.   *Hymn Songs*–H

114. Help Just a Little.

Music from "The Wells of Salvation," new words by Rev. W. A. Spencer.
Wm. J. Kirkpatrick.

1. Brother for Christ's kingdom sighing, Help a little, help a little;
   Help to save the millions dying, Help just a little.
2. Is thy cup made sad by trial? Help a little, help a little;
   Sweeten it with self-denial, Help just a little.
3. Though no wealth to thee is given, Help a little, help a little;
   Sacrifice is gold in heaven, Help just a little.

CHORUS.
Oh, the wrongs that we may righten! Oh, the hearts that we may lighten!
Oh, the skies that we may brighten! Helping just a little.

4 Let us live for one another,
  Help a little, help a little;
  Help to lift each fallen brother,
  Help just a little.

5 Tho' thy life is pressed with sorrow,
  Help a little, help a little;
  Bravely look t'ward God's to-morrow,
  Help just a little.

Copyright, 1885, by John J. Hood.

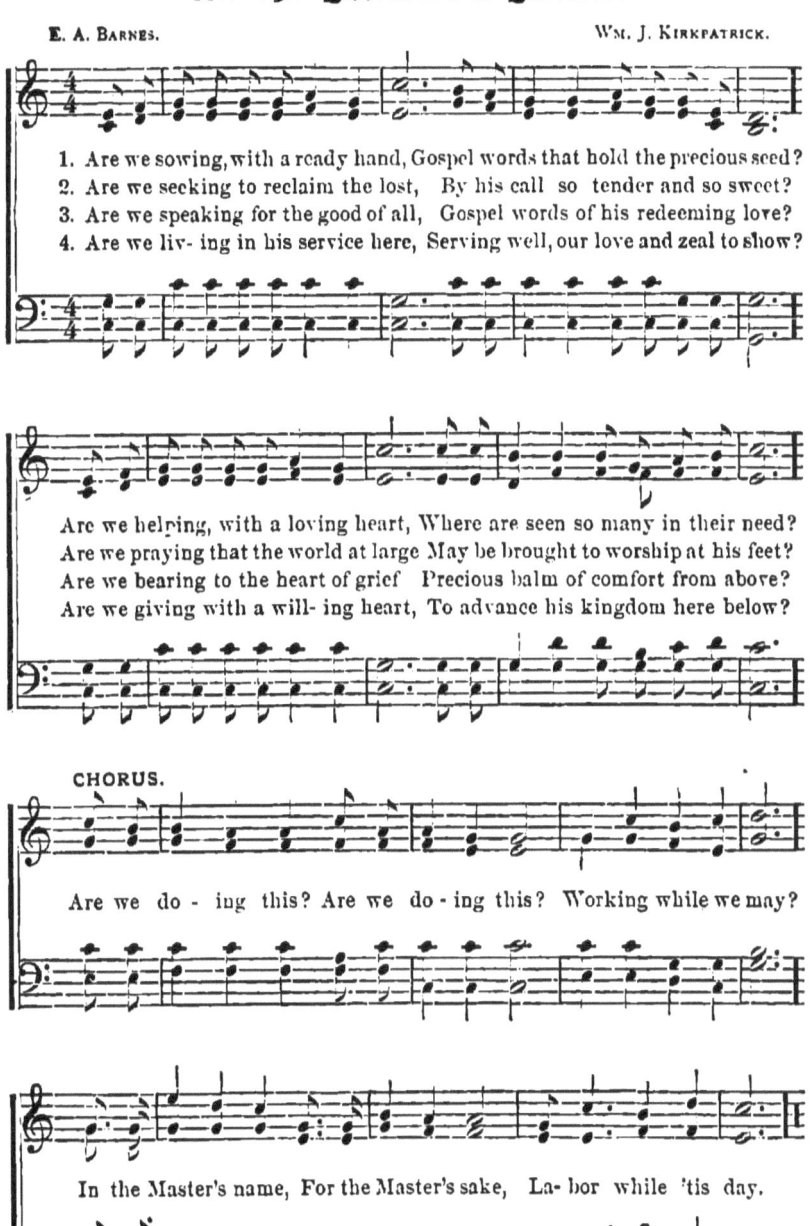

Safe in the Glory Land.

James L. Black.   *Jno. R. Sweney.*

1. In the good old way where the saints have gone, And the King leads on be-fore us, We are travelling home to the heavenly hills, With the day-star shining o'er us.
2. In the good old way like the ransomed throng, Un-to Zi-on now re-turn-ing, We are travelling home at the King's command, And our lamps are trimm'd and burning.
3. In the good old way with a stead-fast faith, In the bonds of love and un-ion, What a joy is ours for the King we see, And with him we hold communion.
4. Tho' our feet must stand on the cold, cold brink Of the Jor-dan's storm-y riv-er, With the King we'll cross to the oth-er side, And we'll sing his praise for-ev-er.

CHORUS.

Travelling home to the mansions fair, Crowns of re-joic-ing and life to wear; O what a shout when we all get there, Safe in the glo-ry land!

Copyright, 1888, by Jno. R. Sweney.

122. All-atoning Blood.

Rev. Jno. O. Foster, A. M.
Jno. R. Sweney.

1. O my Saviour, thou hast washed me In the all-a-ton-ing blood, Thou hast purchased my redemption For the herit-age of God; And the whisper of thy Spirit Thrills my soul with love divine, While the blessed, sweet communion Gives as-surance I am thine.

2. Yes, the Spirit's in-ter-ces-sion Has availed for ev-en me; He has burst the bars asunder, And has set my spirit free. Christ my Lord shall reign for-ev-er In this willing heart of mine; While the light of blessed tokens All a-long my journey shine.

3. Blessed be the cleansing fountain Opened for each guilty soul, Thro' the royal house of David, That the sinner may be whole! Tho' your sins may be as scar-let They shall be as white as snow; Praise his holy name forev-er, Jesus' cleansing power I know!

CHORUS.

I am washed in the blood, I am washed in the blood, I am washed in the blood of the Lamb; When his precious love was

Copyright, 1884, by John J. Hood.

All-atoning Blood.—CONCLUDED.

given I was made an heir of heav'n: I am washed in the blood of the Lamb.

Shall we Meet?

H. L. HASTINGS.   ELISHA S. RICE.

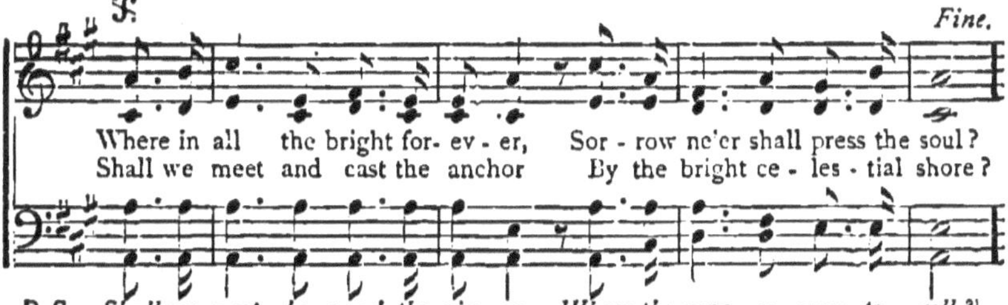

1. Shall we meet beyond the river, Where the surges cease to roll?
2. Shall we meet in that blest harbor, When our stormy voyage is o'er?
Where in all the bright forever, Sorrow ne'er shall press the soul?
Shall we meet and cast the anchor By the bright celestial shore?

D.S. Shall we meet beyond the river, Where the surges cease to roll?

CHORUS.
Shall we meet, shall we meet, Shall we meet beyond the river?

3 Shall we meet in yonder city,
   Where the towers of crystal shine?
   Where the walls are all of jasper,
   Built by workmanship divine?

4 Where the music of the ransomed
   Rolls its harmony around,
   And creation swells the chorus
   With its sweet melodious sound?

5 Shall we meet there many a loved one,
   That was torn from our embrace?
   Shall we listen to their voices,
   And behold them face to face?

6 Shall we meet with Christ our Saviour,
   When he comes to claim his own?
   Shall we know his blessed favor,
   And sit down upon his throne?

Onward and Upward.—CONCLUDED.

up - - ward, Onward unto glory, To the perfect day.
upward, marching upward, upward,

On the Way.

LIZZIE EDWARDS.   JNO. R. SWENEY.

1. Oh, bless the Lord, what joy is mine! What perfect peace thro' grace divine!
2. Oh, bless the Lord, he dwells with me, The voice I hear, the hand I see
3. Oh, bless the Lord for what I know Of heavenly bliss while here below!
4. Oh, bless the Lord 'twill not be long Till I shall join the holy throng,

And now to realms of endless day, Oh, bless the Lord, I'm on the way.
Renew my strength from day to day While home to him I'm on the way.
My trusting heart thro' faith can say, To mansions bright I'm on the way.
And shout and sing thro' endless day, Where ev-'ry tear is wiped a-way.

D.S.—crown to wear in end-less day, Oh, bless the Lord, I'm on the way.

CHORUS.   D.S.

I'm on the way, I'm on the way, In vain the world would bid me stay: A

Copyright, 1890, by Jno. R. Sweney.

The Summer Land.—CONCLUDED.

hail joy's eternal mor-row When the toils of earth shall cease, There to
There, there to hail, there, there to hail,
song, listen to the cho-rus." Praise the Lord the King of kings: Saved by
Hark, hark the song hark, hark the song,
light soon the sky adorn-ing We shall meet with joyful eyes; We shall
Pure holy light, pure ho-ly light,

dwell by the crystal riv-er, Blessed riv-er, blessed riv-er,
There, there to dwell, there, there to dwell, there, there to dwell, there, there to dwell,
grace; glory! halle-lu-jah! Halle-lu-jah! halle-lu-jah!
Saved, saved by grace, saved, saved by grace, saved, saved by grace, saved, saved by grace,
meet by the crystal riv-er, Shining riv-er, shining riv-er;
Yes, we shall meet, yes, we shall meet, yes, we shall meet, yes, we shall meet,

With the Lord happy and for-ev-er, When the toils of earth shall cease.
Dwell with the Lord, dwell with the Lord,
Crowned with love; glory! halle-lu-jah! Praise the mighty King of kings."
Crowned, crowned with love, crowned, crowned with love,
On its banks meet no more to sev-er, Look beyond with joyful eyes.
There on its banks, there on its banks,

F. J. C.   **The Prince of Peace.**   Tune above.

1 'Twas a night of long ago when all were
   sleeping, sleeping, sleeping, [keeping,
When the lonely silent stars a watch were
   Softly o'er the dreaming, dreaming earth;
Floods of light bursting forth in glory,
   (Pure floods of light, pure floods of light, etc.,)
Brightest glory, brightest glory,
Harp and voice told the joyful story
   (Sweet harp and voice, sweet harp and voice,)
Of his birth the Prince of Peace.

Cho.—He has come; hail the lovely stranger,
   (Yes, he has come, yes, he has come, etc.,)
Lovely stranger, lovely stranger,
Lo, the babe cradled in a manger
   (O blessed babe, O blessed babe,)
Is the King and Prince of Peace.

2 See the rosy blushing morn again is
   breaking, breaking, breaking,
And the melody of song again is waking
   Music in the hearts of all to-day;
Praise the Lord, come with happy voices,
   (Praise, praise the Lord, praise, praise the Lord,)
Happy voices, happy voices,
Praise the Lord, how the world rejoices,
   (Praise, praise the Lord, praise, praise the Lord,)
At his birth the Prince of Peace.

3 Hark the merry silver bells are sweetly
   ringing, ringing, ringing,
And the multitude of angels now are singing
   Glory in the highest evermore;
Sing aloud, glory! hallelujah!
   (Sing, sing aloud, sing, sing aloud, etc.,)
Hallelujah! hallelujah!
Sing aloud, glory! hallelujah!
   (Sing, sing aloud, sing, sing aloud,)
At his birth the Prince of Peace.

From "Hood's Carols for— —Christmas, No. 6," by per.

134. Jesus will Welcome Me There.

FANNY J. CROSBY.
JNO. R. SWENEY.

1. Over the riv-er they call me, Friends that are dear to my heart;
2. Over the riv-er they call me, Hark, 'tis their voices I hear,
3. Over the riv-er, how love-ly, There is no sorrow nor night;
4. Over the riv-er they call me, Watching with glad, beaming eyes;

Soon shall I meet them in glo-ry, Never, no nev-er to part.
Borne on the wings of the twi-light, Murmuring soft-ly and clear.
There they are walking with Je-sus, Clothed in his garment of light.
O-ver the riv-er I'm com-ing, Joyful my spir-it re-plies.

CHORUS.

O-ver the riv-er to E-den, Home to their dwelling so fair;
An-gels will car-ry me safe-ly, Je-sus will welcome me there.

Copyright, 1892, by Jno. R. Sweney.

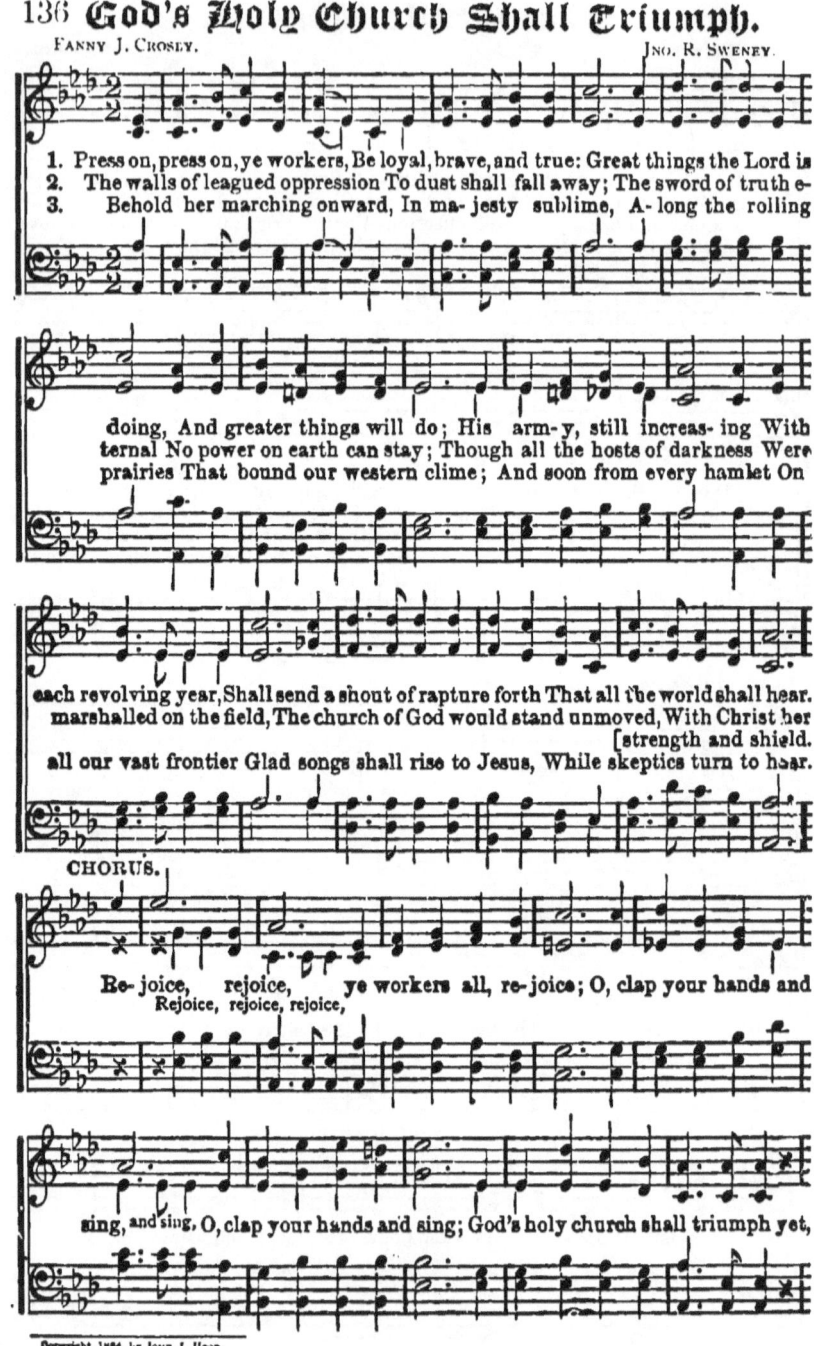

God's Holy Church.—CONCLUDED.

triumph yet, triumph yet, And he shall reign our King, shall reign our King.

Light after Darkness.

JNO. R. SWENEY.

DUET.

1. Light after darkness, Gain after loss, Strength after weakness, Crown after cross, Sweet after bitter, Song after fears, Home after wandering, Praise after tears.
2. Sheaves after sowing, Sun after rain, Sight after mystery, Peace after pain, Joy after sorrow, Calm after blast, Rest after weariness,—Sweet rest at last.
3. Near after distant, Gleam after gloom, Love after loneliness, Life after tomb; After long agony, Rapture of bliss; Right was the pathway Leading to this!

From "Goodly Pearls," by per.

140. What a Gath'ring that will be.

J. H. K.   "Gather my saints together unto me."—Ps. l. 5.   J. H. Kurzenknabe.

1. At the sounding of the trumpet, when the saints are gather'd home, We will greet each other by the crystal sea, With the friends and all the lov'd ones there a-waiting us to come, What a gath'ring of the faithful that will be!
2. When the angel of the Lord proclaims that time shall be no more, We shall gather, and the saved and ransom'd see, Then to meet again together, on the bright ce-lestial shore, What a gath'ring of the faithful that will be!
3. At the great and final judg-ment, when the hidden comes to light, When the Lord in all his glory we shall see; At the bidding of our Saviour, "Come, ye blessed to my right, What a gath'ring of the faithful that will be!
4. When the golden harps are sounding, and the angel bands proclaim, In tri-umphant strains the glorious jubilee; Then to meet and join to sing the song of Moses and the Lamb, What a gath'ring of the faithful that will be!

CHORUS.

What a gath - - - - 'ring, gath - - 'ring, At the sounding of the glorious jubi - lee! What a gath - 'ring,
What a gath'ring of the loved ones when we'll meet with one an-oth-er, jubilee! What a gath'ring when the friends and all the

From "Song Treasury," by per.

What A Gath'ring, etc.—CONCLUDED.

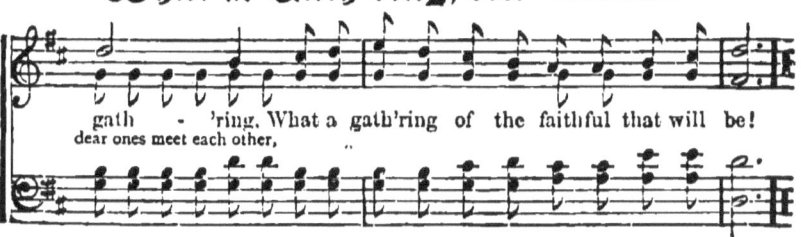

gath - 'ring. What a gath'ring of the faithful that will be!
dear ones meet each other,

When shall We all Meet again?

Arr. by L. H. Edmunds.   Adapted and arr. by Wm. J. Kirkpatrick.

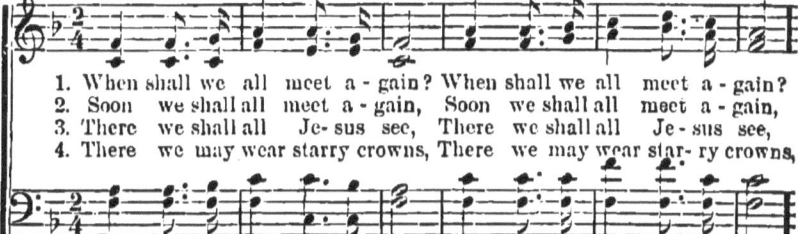

1. When shall we all meet a-gain? When shall we all meet a-gain?
2. Soon we shall all meet a-gain, Soon we shall all meet a-gain,
3. There we shall all Je-sus see, There we shall all Je-sus see,
4. There we may wear starry crowns, There we may wear star-ry crowns,

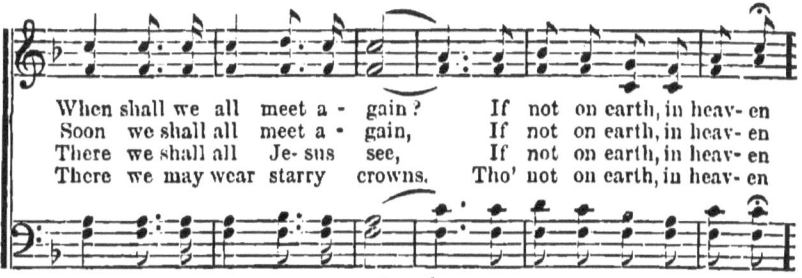

When shall we all meet a - gain?   If not on earth, in heav-en
Soon we shall all meet a - gain,   If not on earth, in heav-en
There we shall all Je-sus see,   If not on earth, in heav-en
There we may wear starry crowns.   Tho' not on earth, in heav-en

Shall we all meet a-gain?
We shall all meet a-gain.
We shall all Je-sus see.
We may all wear bright crowns.

5 ‖: There we shall meet friends we love, :‖
    When we get home to heaven
    We shall meet friends we love.

6 ‖: There we shall *never* part again, :‖
    When we get home to heaven
    We shall *never* part again.

7 ‖: There we shall *never* say good-by, :‖
    When we get home to heaven
    We shall *never* say good-by.

Copyright, 1891, by Wm. J. Kirkpatrick.

142. When the Curtains are Lifted.

Mrs Annie Wittenmeyer.
Wm. J. Kirkpatrick.

1. When the curtains are lifted, Oh, what shall I see? Will my Lord with his angels Be waiting for me? Will he welcome my coming, And crown me his own, With the saints of all a-ges, That cir-cle his throne.
2. Will the heaven-ly city Burst full on my sight; And the throne of his glory, That giveth it light? Will the feet torn and weary Reach pavements of gold, And the eyes red with weeping, The Saviour behold?
3. Now the future is hidden, I see but a pace, Yet it may be I'm nearing The end of the race; It will matter but little What changes may come, If my Lord with his angels Shall welcome me home.
4. When his glorified presence Shall gladden mine eyes, I'll be chang'd and be like him, And with him arise; And the hands hard with labor A victor's palm raise; And the lips tuned to sorrow Sing anthems of praise.

CHORUS.

(1, 2, 3.) When the curtains are lifted, Oh, what shall I see? Will my Lord and his angels be waiting for me, Be wait - - ing, be wait - - ing, Will my Lord and his angels be waiting for me?

(4.) When the curtains are lifted, Oh, this shall I see, That my Lord and his angels are waiting for me, Are wait - - ing, are wait - - ing, That my Lord and his angels are waiting for me?

Be waiting for me? be waiting for me?
Are waiting for me? are waiting for me?

Copyright, 1891, by Wm. J. Kirkpatrick.

Building Day by Day.—CONCLUDED.

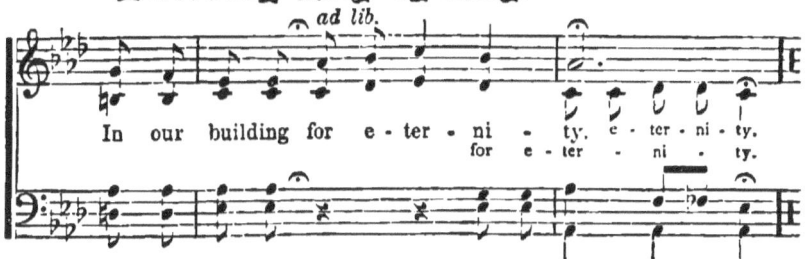

In our building for e-ter-ni-ty, e-ter-ni-ty.
for e-ter-ni-ty.

Wash Me, O Lamb of God.

H. B. BEEGLE. WM. J. KIRKPATRICK.

May be used as a Duett.

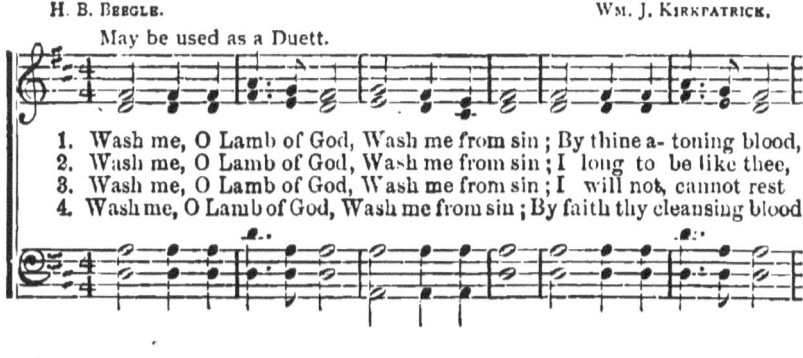

1. Wash me, O Lamb of God, Wash me from sin; By thine a-toning blood,
2. Wash me, O Lamb of God, Wash me from sin; I long to be like thee,
3. Wash me, O Lamb of God, Wash me from sin; I will not, cannot rest
4. Wash me, O Lamb of God, Wash me from sin; By faith thy cleansing blood

Oh, make me clean; Purge me from every stain, Let me thine image gain,
All pure within; Now let the crimson tide Shed from thy wounded side
Till pure within; All human skill is vain, But thou canst cleanse each stain,
Now makes me clean. So near thou art to me, So sweet my rest in thee,

In love and mercy reign O'er all within.
Be to my heart applied, And make me clean.
Till not a spot remain, Made wholly clean.
Oh, blessed purity! Saved, saved from sin.

5 Wash me, O Lamb of God,
  Wash me from sin;
Thou, while I trust in thee,
  Wilt keep me clean;
Each day to thee I bring
Heart, life, yea, everything;
Saved while to thee I cling,
  Saved from all sin.

Copyright, 1893, by Wm. J. Kirkpatrick.

Hymn Songs-K

Toiling for Thee.—CONCLUDED. 149

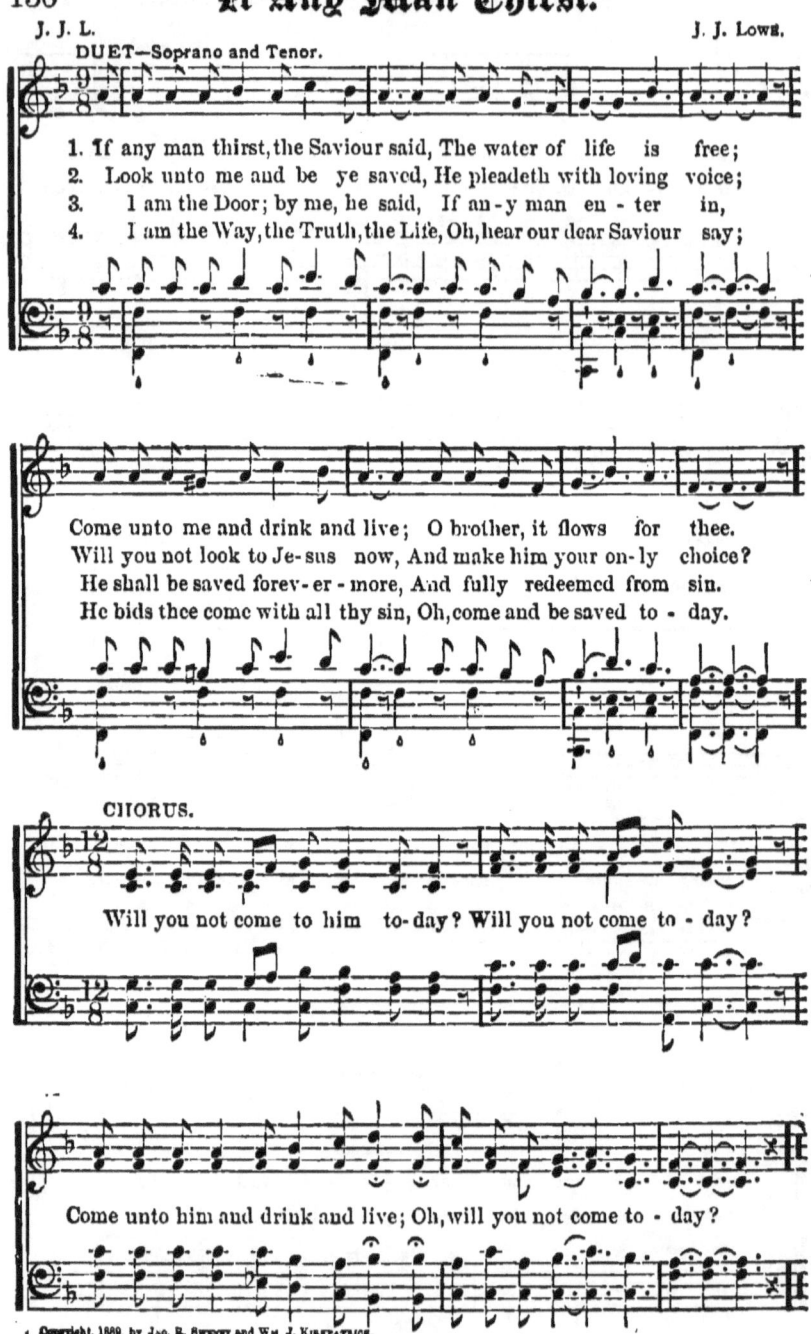

It Must be Told.—CONCLUDED.

sto - ry, ... O Christian, must be told.
sto - ry, wondrous sto - ry, oft- en sweetly told.

Brightest Day.

L. F. L.   For "Children's Day." Service.   L. F. LINDSAY.

1. Another year has passed away, Since last we met on Children's Day;
2. Our teachers here to-day we greet, And with them bow at Jesus' feet,
3. Since last we met on Children's Day Some have gone the heav'nly way,
4. We'll trust him still for years to come, And hope to meet when years are done,

Each Sabbath filled with ho - ly song, As we have mingled with the throng.
To thank him as we thus draw near, For all the blessings of the year.
To sing with him a glad new hymn: We know our dear Saviour let them in
'Mid flow'rs, in robes of white ar - ray, Where ev'ry day is Children's Day.

D.S.—As flow'rs we bring our hearts to thee, Make them, our Saviour, pure and free.

CHORUS.   D.S.

Brightest day, beau-ti-ful day, This is hap-py Children's Day;

Copyright, 1895, by L. F. Lindsay.

154. The Stranger at the Door.

Rev. iii. 20.   T. C. O'Kane.

1. Behold a stranger at the door, He gently knocks—has knocked before, Has wait-ed long, is wait-ing still; You treat no oth-er friend so ill.
2. O love-ly at-titude,—he stands With melting heart and open hands; O matchless kindness, and he shows This matchless kindness to his foes.
3. But will he prove a friend indeed? He will,—the very friend you need; The friend of sin-ners? Yes, 'tis he, With garments dyed on Cal-va-ry.

CHORUS.
Oh, let the dear Saviour come in, He'll cleanse the heart from sin; Oh, keep him no more out at the door, But let the dear Saviour come in.

4 Rise, touched with gratitude divine,
Turn out his enemy and thine;
That soul-destroying monster, Sin,
And let the heavenly Stranger in.

5 Admit him, ere his anger burn,—
His feet, departed, ne'er return;
Admit him, or the hour's at hand
You'll at his door rejected stand.

By permission.

Whisper to Me.

L. H. Edmunds.
James N. Clemmer.

1. Jesus my Saviour, Whisper to me, Tell me of mercy, Boundless and free; Mercy that sought me Thro' the dark night, Wondrously brought me To walk in the light.
2. Jesus my Saviour, Whisper to me, Tenderly draw me Nearer to thee; Oh, let thy Spirit, Heavenly Dove, Dwelling within me, Reveal thy great love.
3. Jesus my Saviour, Whisper to me, Tell me of mansions Over the sea; There blessed voices Joyfully blend, There shall I praise thee, Where songs never end.

CHORUS.

Bless-ed communion! Lean-ing on thee; Jesus my Saviour, Oh, whisper to me.

Blessed, blessed Leaning, leaning on thee; Jesus, Jesus my Saviour,

Copyright, 1895, by Jno. R. Sweney.

156. Beautiful Robes.

E. E. Hewitt.
Wm. J. Kirkpatrick.

Not too fast.

1. We shall walk with him in white, In that country pure and bright, Where shall enter naught that may defile; Where the day-beam ne'er declines, For the blessed light that shines Is the glo-ry of the Saviour's smile.
2. We shall walk with him in white, Where faith yields to blissful sight, When the beauty of the King we see; Holding converse full and sweet, In fel-lowship complete; Waking songs of ho-ly mel-o-dy.
3. We shall walk with him in white, By the fountains of delight, Where the Lamb his ransomed ones shall lead, For his blood shall wash each stain, Till no spot of sin remain, And the soul for-ev-ermore is freed.

CHORUS.

Beau - - tiful robes, .. Beau - - tiful robes, ..
Beautiful robes, beautiful robes, Beautiful robes, beautiful robes,

Beau - - - ti-ful robes we then shall wear, ..
Beau-ti-ful robes we then shall wear, Beau-ti-ful robes we then shall wear,

Copyright, 1890, by Wm. J. Kirkpatrick.

Beautiful Robes.—CONCLUDED.

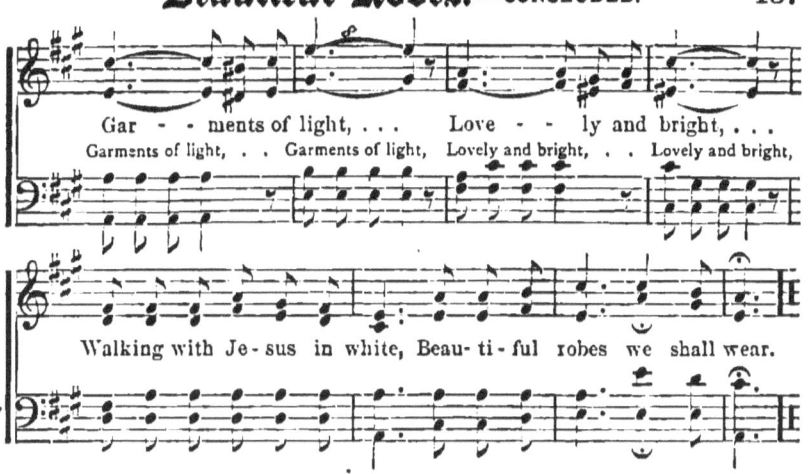

Gar - - ments of light, . . . Love - - ly and bright, . . .
Garments of light, . . Garments of light, Lovely and bright, . . Lovely and bright,
Walking with Jesus in white, Beautiful robes we shall wear.

Follow All the Way.

Geo. W. Collins.   Arr. by W. J. K.

1. I have heard my Saviour calling, I have heard my Saviour calling,
2. Tho' he leads me thro' the valley, Tho' he leads me thro' the valley,
3. Tho' he leads me thro' the garden, Tho' he leads me thro' the garden,

Cho.—Where he leads me I will follow, Where he leads me I will follow,

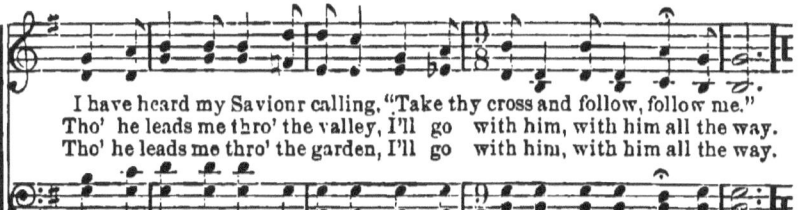

I have heard my Saviour calling, "Take thy cross and follow, follow me."
Tho' he leads me thro' the valley, I'll go with him, with him all the way.
Tho' he leads me thro' the garden, I'll go with him, with him all the way.

Copyright, 1891, by Wm. J. Kirkpatrick.

Where he leads me I will follow, I'll go with him, with him all the way.

4 ‖: Tho' the path be dark and dreary, :‖
    I'll go with him, with him all the way.

5 ‖: Tho' he leads me to the conflict, :‖
    I'll go with him, with him all the way.

6 ‖: Tho' he leads through fiery trials, :‖
    I'll go with him, with him all the way.

7 ‖: I will follow on to know him, :‖
    He's my Saviour, Saviour, Brother, Friend.

8 ‖: He will give me grace and glory, :‖
    He will keep me, keep me all the way.

9 ‖: O 'tis sweet to follow Jesus, :‖
    And be with him, with him all the way.

Blessed Refuge.

159

Fanny J. Crosby. Mrs. Rev. J. G. Wilson.

ALTO OR BASS SOLO.

1. Blessed refuge of the soul, With thy love o'ershadow me;
2. Blessed refuge, mine a-lone, While in fervent pray'r I bend;
3. Blessed refuge, ev-er near, Precious balm for all my woes;

Cho.—Blessed refuge of the soul, With thy love o'ershadow me;

Still the raging waves con-trol, Keep my anchor firm on thee.
From thy bright ce-les-tial throne Let the star of faith descend,
What have I to ask or fear While I still on thee re-pose?

Still the raging waves con-trol, Keep my anchor firm on thee.

Gent-ly o'er the ocean's foam Cheer my heart and guide my way;
May its pure and sacred rays, Breaking thro' the clouds of night,
Soon with angels I shall rise Far above this changeful shore,

D. C. Chorus.

Till I hear thy welcome home, Safe within the gates of day.
Fill my waking thoughts with praise, Till I hail the morning light.
Where the dawning never dies, And the darkness comes no more.

Copyright, 1883, by Jno. R. Sweney.

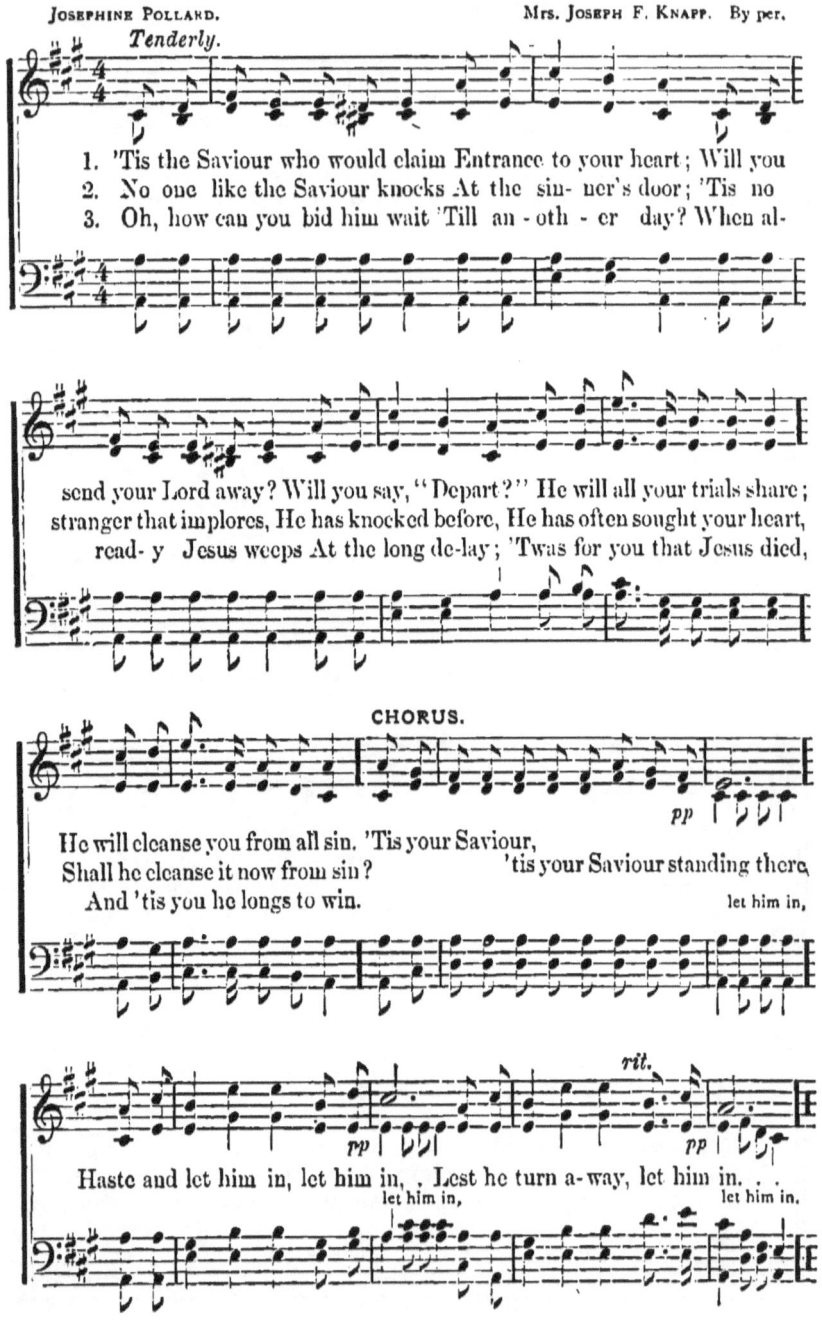

Send Me. 161

Rev. Daniel March, D. D.   Jno. R. Sweney.

1. Hark, the voice of Je-sus, cry-ing, Who will go and work to-day?
2. If you cannot cross the o-cean, And the heathen lands explore,
3. If you have not gifts and grac-es, If you cannot preach like Paul,
4. Let none hear you i-dly say-ing, "There is nothing I can do,"

Cho.—Hark, the voice of Je-sus, cry-ing, Who will go and work to-day?

Fields are white, and harvests wait-ing, Who will bear the sheaves away?
You can find the heathen near-er, You can help them at your door.
You can tell the love of Je-sus, You can say he died for all.
While the souls of men are dy-ing, And the Master calls for you.

Fields are white, and harvests waiting,—Who will bear the sheaves away?

Key D.

Long and loud the Master call-eth, Rich rewards he offers free:
If you cannot give your thousands You can give the widow's mite,
If you cannot rouse the wick-ed With the judgement's dread alarms,
Take the task he gives you glad-ly, Let his work your pleasure be;

Who will answer, gladly say-ing, "Here am I, send me, send me."
And the least you give for Je-sus Will be precious in his sight.
You can lead the lit-tle child-ren To the Saviour's waiting arms.
Answer quickly when he call-eth: "Here am I, send me, send me."

Hymn Songs—L From "Gems of Praise," by per.

3 Can my lips be mute, or my heart be sad,
When the gracious Master hath made me glad?
When he points where the many mansions be,
And sweetly says, 'There is one for thee'?

4 I shall catch the gleam of its jasper wall
When I come to the gloom of the evenfall,
For I know that the shadows, dreary and dim,
Have a path of light that will lead to him.

From "Gems of Praise," by per.

Fill Me Now.

Rev. E. H. Stokes, D.D.   Jno. R. Sweney.

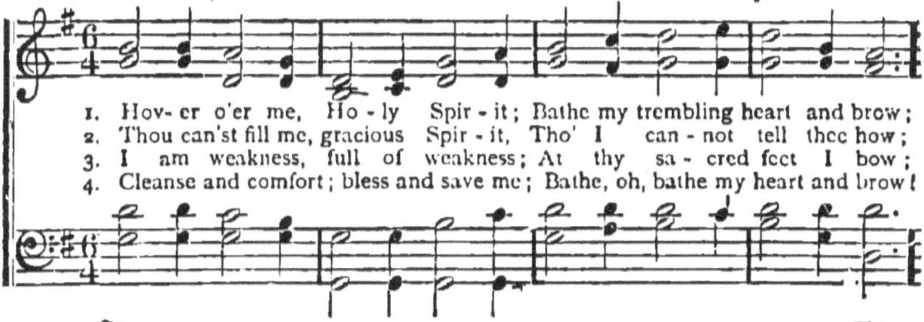

1. Hov-er o'er me, Ho-ly Spir-it; Bathe my trembling heart and brow;
2. Thou can'st fill me, gracious Spir-it, Tho' I can-not tell thee how;
3. I am weakness, full of weakness; At thy sa-cred feet I bow;
4. Cleanse and comfort; bless and save me; Bathe, oh, bathe my heart and brow!

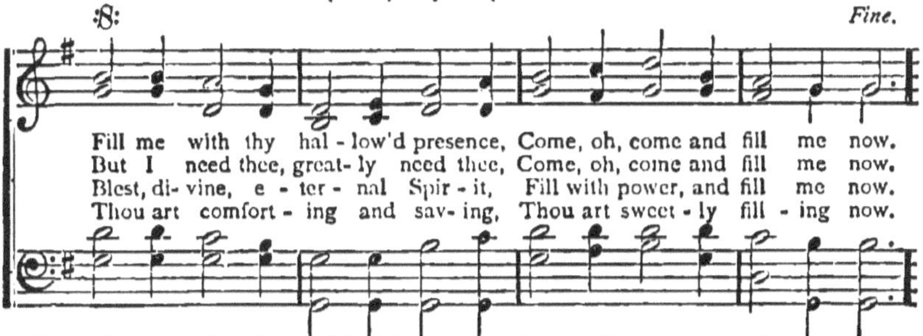

Fill me with thy hal-low'd presence, Come, oh, come and fill me now.
But I need thee, great-ly need thee, Come, oh, come and fill me now.
Blest, di-vine, e-ter-nal Spir-it, Fill with power, and fill me now.
Thou art comfort-ing and sav-ing, Thou art sweet-ly fill-ing now.

D.S. Fill me with thy hal-low'd presence,—Come, oh, come and fill me now.

CHORUS.   *D.S.*

Fill me now, fill me now, Ho-ly Spir-it, and fill me now;

COPYRIGHT, 1879, by JOHN J. HOOD.

166. Just Ahead.

Edgar Page. Cho. by H. L. G.
H. L. Gilmour.

1. 'Mid the toil and the bat-tle I think of my home, Where the sound of life's conflict can nevermore come, Where the angel of peace spreads his wings o'er the scene, And e-ter-ni-ty's sea is all calm and se-rene.
2. By the bank of life's riv-er our loved we shall greet, With them shall rejoice in a rapture complete, Shall join in the song that the glo-ri-fied sing, While the arches of heav-en shall tremble and ring.
3. There cher-ubs ef-ful-gent and ser-aphs that blaze May join in our anthem of rapturous praise; And the Son that was given the world to redeem, Shall be of our joy-ing and praising the theme.
4. As year af-ter year shall fly swift-ly a-way, And yet but begun is e-ter-ni-ty's day, While springs of new pleasure de-light-eth the soul, While on-ward, yet on-ward, the ag-es shall roll.
5. Pre-pare, then, ye faith-ful, to en-ter your land, The mansion prepared by the Saviour's own hand, 'Tis read-y, now waiting, so beauteous and fair! Then bind on your san-dals, we soon shall be there.

CHORUS.

Just a-head, just a-head, a-head, I see the pearl-y gates unfold, And hear the harps of shining gold, Where blood-bought saints the

Copyright, 1889, by H. L. Gilmour.

Just Ahead.—CONCLUDED.

new song sing To him who redeemed us, our bless-ed King.

Nearer to Thee.

MARTHA J. LANKTON.   WM. J. KIRKPATRICK.

1. When doubt and conflict weigh me down, and | clouds be-fore me | rise,
2. When joys that once I thought so true Have | lost each balm-y | sweet,
3. While day by day I journey on To . . . . | reach that world sub- | lime,

Whose gath'ring gloom and deep'ning shade With | sor-row fills mine | eyes,
And withered hopes, like summer flowers, Lie | crushed beneath my | feet,
That stands in perfect loveliness Be - - - | yond the shore of | time;

'Tis then I lift my fainting soul In . . . | prayer that I may | be
With quivering lip and yearning heart I | pray on bend-ed | knee,
My faith looks up and softly breathes The | prayer so dear to | me,

Lento.

Near - - er, my God, to thee, Near - - er to thee.

Copyright, 1887, by John J. Hood.

Leaning on the Everlasting Arms. 171

Rev. E. A. Hoffman. A. J. Showalter.

1. What a fel-lowship, what a joy divine, Leaning on the ev-er-lasting arms; What a bless-ed-ness, What a peace is mine,
2. Oh, how sweet to walk in this pilgrim way, Leaning on the ev-er-lasting arms; Oh, how bright the path grows from day to day,
3. What have I to dread, what have I to fear, Leaning on the ev-er-lasting arms? I have bless-ed peace with my Lord so near,

REFRAIN.

Lean-ing on the ev-er-last-ing arms, Lean-ing, lean-ing, Safe and se-cure from all a-larms; Lean-ing, lean-ing, Leaning on the ev-er-lasting arms.
Lean-ing on Je-sus, Lean-ing on Je-sus, Lean-ing on Je-sus, lean-ing on Je-sus,

By per. A. J. Showalter

The Bethlehem Shepherds.—CONCLUDED.

FROM HOUSE TO HOUSE.

Tune, "What a Friend We Have in Jesus."—Key F.

1 Go, ye workers in God's vineyard,
　Go, ye heralds of the cross;
Go, invite the lost to Jesus,
　Go, you will not suffer loss,
Go, for God will give you courage,
　Go, you will not be alone;
Go, his arm will be around you,
　Go, for him, to every home.

2 You may meet with many trials,
　You may sometimes meet rebuff;
You may find the way unpleasant,
　You must pray for grace enough.

You must work and do the bidding—
　You have his command to "go;"
You must never be discouraged,
　You will overcome the foe.

3 Grant us, Lord, thy heavenly blessing,
　Give us now grace from above,
House to house, for visitation,
　In thy name we'll go in love,
Epworth Leaguers and Endeav'rers,
　Pastors, Teachers, Scholars, all,
Are united in this service
　On us richest blessings fall.
　　　　　　　　—L. F. Lindsay.

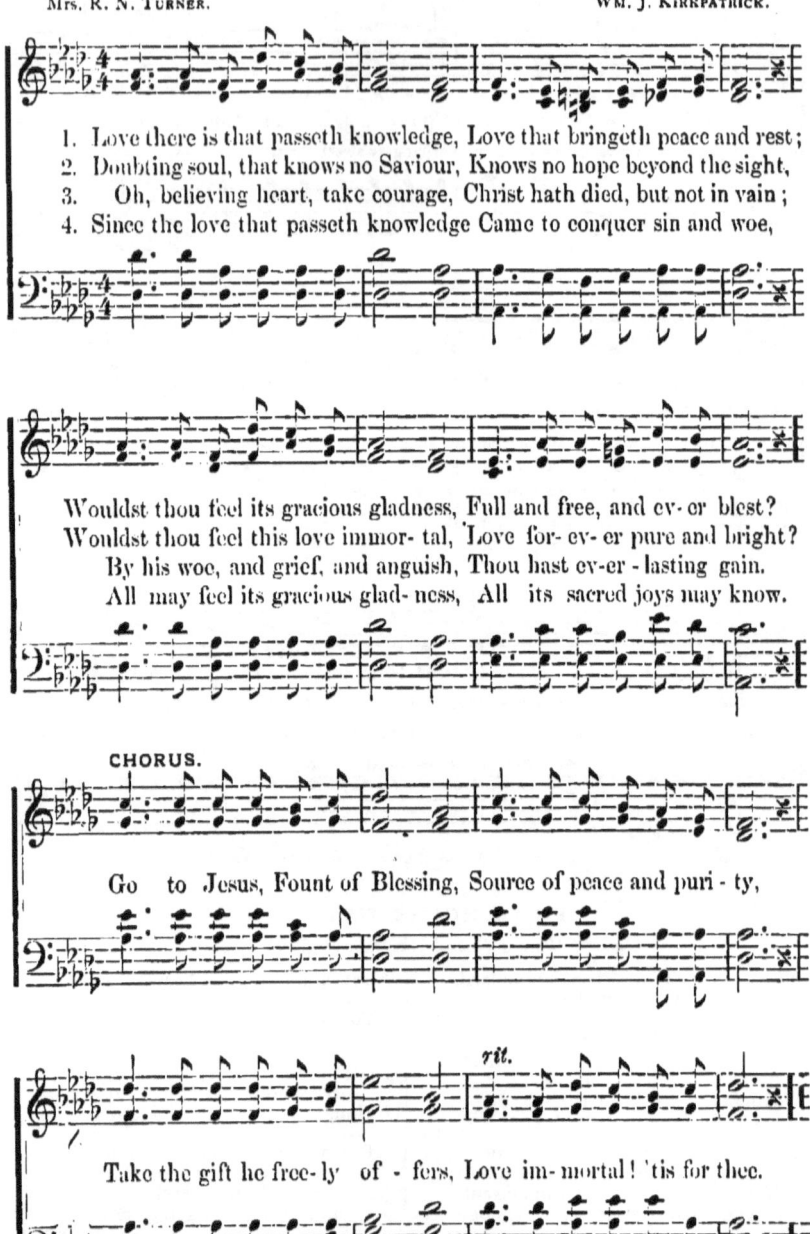

Make Me a Blessing To-day.

"Lord bless me, and make me a blessing."—Rev. D. B. Updegraff.

Rev. H. J. Zelley.   H. L. Gilmour.

1. I do not ask to choose my path, Lord, lead me in thy way;
2. Around me, Lord, are sin-ful men, Who scorn and dis-o-bey;
3. To those who once thy love have known, But now are far a-stray;
4. Some saints of thine are in distress, And for thy ful-ness pray;
5. If thou hast an-y errand, Lord, Send me, and I'll o-bey;

Inspire each thought and prompt each word, And make me a blessing to-day.
Use me to win them from their sins, And make me a blessing to-day.
Help me to lead them back to thee, And make me a blessing to-day.
Oh, let me go and help them Lord, And make me a blessing to-day.
Use me in an-y way thou wilt, And make me a blessing to-day.

CHORUS.

Bless me, Lord, and make me a blessing, I'll gladly thy message convey;

Use me to help some poor, needy soul, And make me a blessing to-day.

Copyright, 1894, by H. L. Gilmour.

Victory Through Grace.—CONCLUDED.

Yet to the true and the faithful Vict'ry is promised through grace.

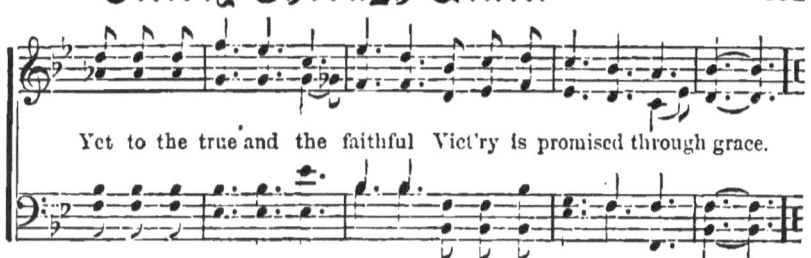

Holy, holy, holy.

REGINALD HEBER. Tune, NICEA. 11, 12, 10.

1. Ho-ly, ho-ly, ho-ly, Lord God Almight-y! Ear-ly in the morn-ing our song shall rise to thee; Ho-ly, ho-ly, ho-ly, mer-ci-ful and might-y, God in Three Persons, blessed Trin-i-ty!
2. Ho-ly, ho-ly, ho-ly! all the saints adore thee, Casting down their gold-en crowns around the glas-sy sea; Cher-u-bim and seraphim falling down before thee, Which wert, and art, and evermore shalt be.
3. Ho-ly, ho-ly, ho-ly! tho' the darkness hide thee, Tho' the eye of sin-ful man thy glo-ry may not see; On-ly thou art ho-ly! there is none be-side thee, Per-fect in power, in love, and pur-i-ty.
4. Ho-ly, ho-ly, ho-ly, Lord God Almight-y! All thy works shall praise thy name, in earth, and sky, and sea; Ho-ly, ho-ly, ho-ly, mer-ci-ful and might-y, God in Three Persons, blessed Trin-i-ty!

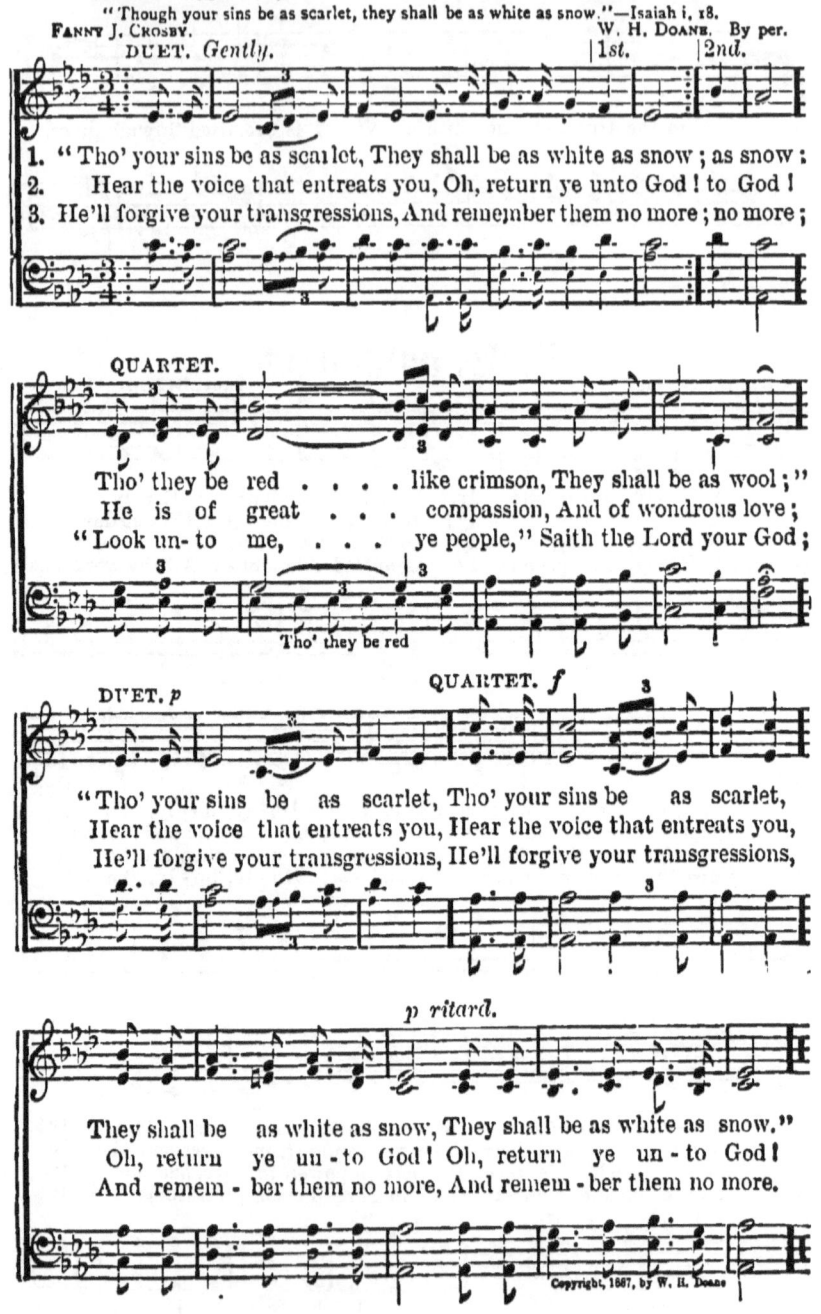

186. Onward, Christian Soldiers!

SABINE BARING-GOULD.　　　　　　　　　　　Tune, ONWARD. 6, 5.

1. Onward, Christian soldiers! Marching as to war, With the cross of Jesus Go-ing on be-fore. Christ, the royal Mas-ter, Leads against the foe; Forward into bat-tle, See, his banners go!
2. At the sign of triumph Satan's host doth flee; On, then, Christian soldiers, On to vic-to-ry! Hell's foundations qiv-er At the shout of praise; Brothers, lift your voices, Loud your anthems raise.
3. Like a mighty army Moves the Church of God; Brothers, we are treading Where the saints have trod; We are not di-vid-ed, All one bo-dy we, One in hope and doctrine, One in chari-ty.

CHORUS.

Onward, Christian soldiers! Marching as to war, With the cross of Je-sus Going on be-fore.

4 Crowns and thrones may perish,
　Kingdoms rise and wane,
　But the Church of Jesus
　　Constant will remain;
　Gates of hell can never
　　'Gainst that Church prevail;
　We have Christ's own promise,
　　And that cannot fail.

5 Onward, then, ye people!
　Join our happy throng,
　Blend with ours your voices
　　In the triumph-song;
　Glory, laud, and honor
　　Unto Christ the King,
　This through countless ages
　　Men and angels sing.

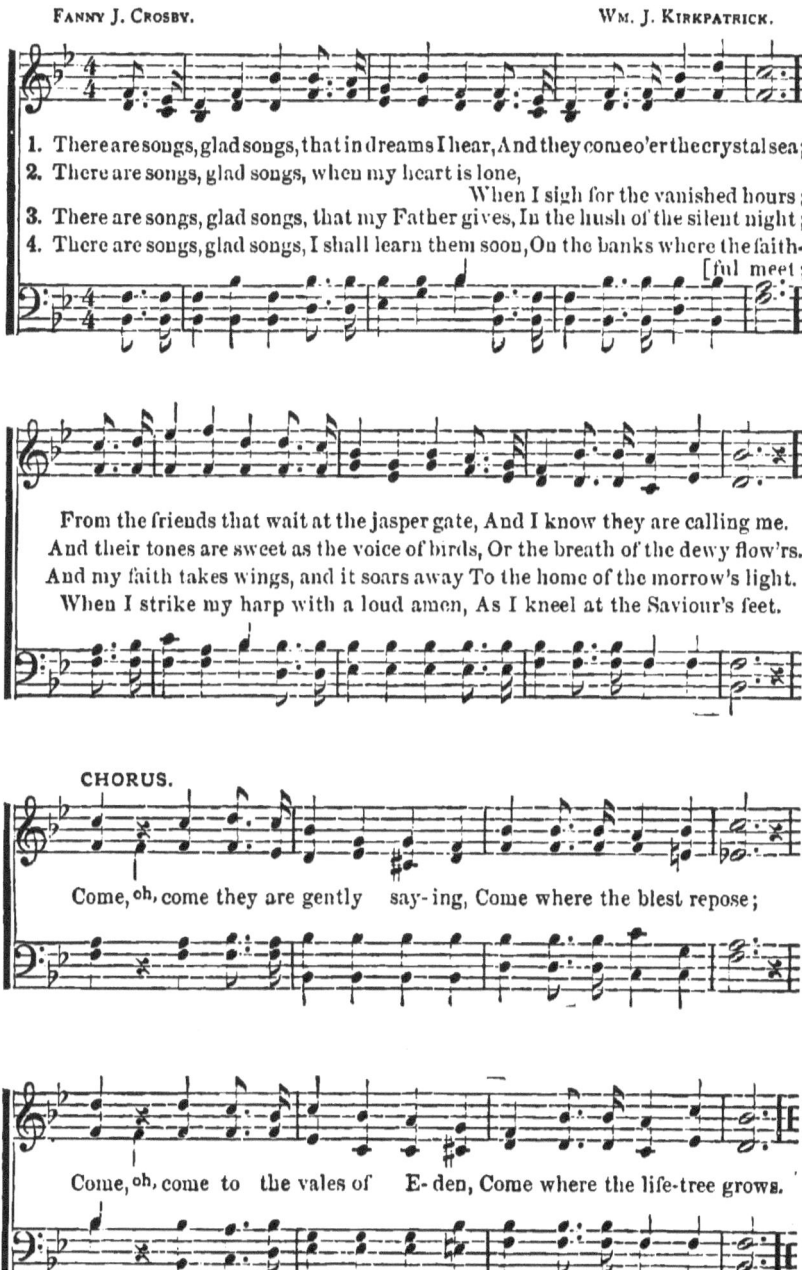

feel, Tell it out, tell it out with glad - ness.
world the joy you feel,

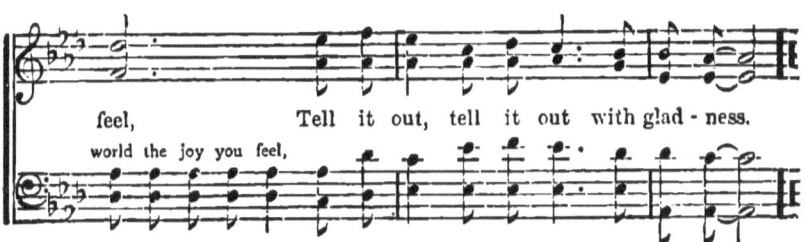

Lord, I'm Coming Home.

W. J. K. Wm. J. Kirkpatrick.

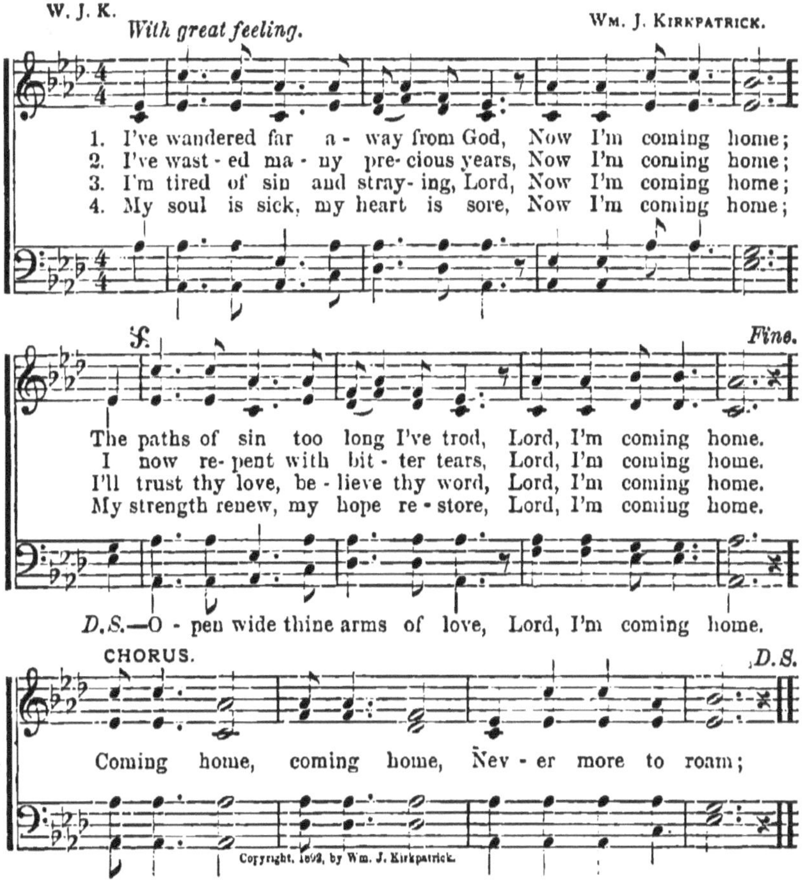
With great feeling.
1. I've wandered far a - way from God, Now I'm coming home;
2. I've wast - ed ma - ny pre- cious years, Now I'm coming home;
3. I'm tired of sin and stray - ing, Lord, Now I'm coming home;
4. My soul is sick, my heart is sore, Now I'm coming home;
Fine.
The paths of sin too long I've trod, Lord, I'm coming home.
I now re - pent with bit - ter tears, Lord, I'm coming home.
I'll trust thy love, be - lieve thy word, Lord, I'm coming home.
My strength renew, my hope re - store, Lord, I'm coming home.
D.S.—O - pen wide thine arms of love, Lord, I'm coming home.
CHORUS.
D.S.
Coming home, coming home, Nev - er more to roam;
Copyright, 1892, by Wm. J. Kirkpatrick.

5 My only hope, my only plea,
Now I'm coming home,
That Jesus died, and died for me,
Lord, I'm coming home.

6 I need his cleansing blood I know,
Now I'm coming home;
Oh, wash me whiter than the snow,
Lord, I'm coming home.

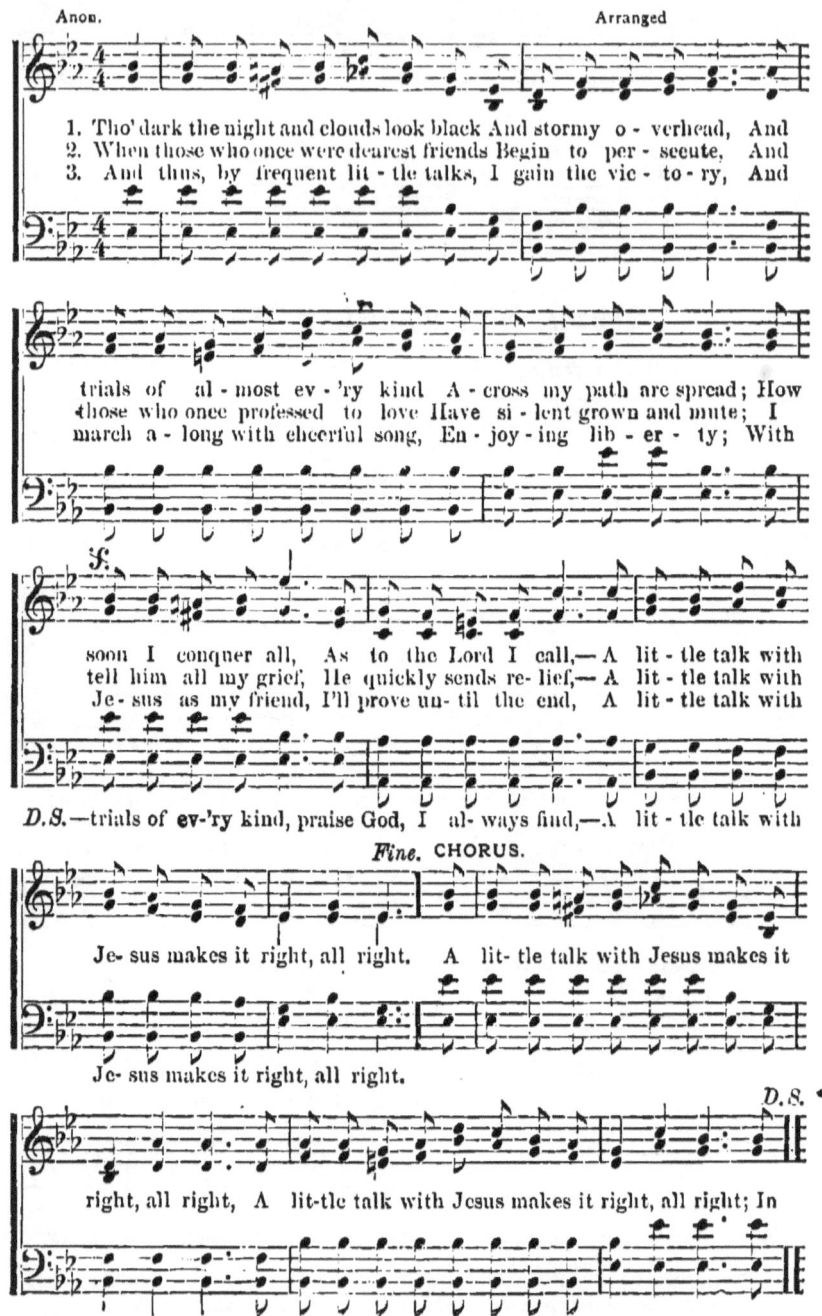

192. Jesus Leads.

"And when he putteth forth his own sheep, he goeth before them, and the sheep follow him: for they know his voice."—John x: 4.

JOHN R. CLEMENTS.   JNO. R. SWENEY.

Andante.

1. Like a shepherd, tender, true, Je-sus leads, ... Je-sus leads, ..
Dai-ly finds us pastures new, Je-sus leads, ... Je-sus leads; ..
If thick mists are o'er the way, ... Or the flock 'mid danger feeds, ..
He will watch them lest they stray, Je-sus leads, ... Je-sus leads.

2. All a-long life's rugged road Je-sus leads, ... Je-sus leads, ..
Till we reach yon blest a-bode, Je-sus leads, ... Je-sus leads; ..
All the way, before, he's trod, And he now the flock precedes, ..
Safe in-to the fold of God Je-sus leads, ... Je-sus leads.

3. Thro' the sun-lit ways of life Je-sus leads, ... Je-sus leads, ..
Thro' the war-ings and the strife Je-sus leads, ... Je-sus leads; ..
When we reach the Jordan's tide, Where life's bound-'ry-line re-cedes, ..
He will spread the waves a-side, Je-sus leads, ... Je-sus leads.

Copyright, 1893, by Jno. R. Sweney.

We Walk by Faith.

Fanny J. Crosby. Wm. J. Kirkpatrick.

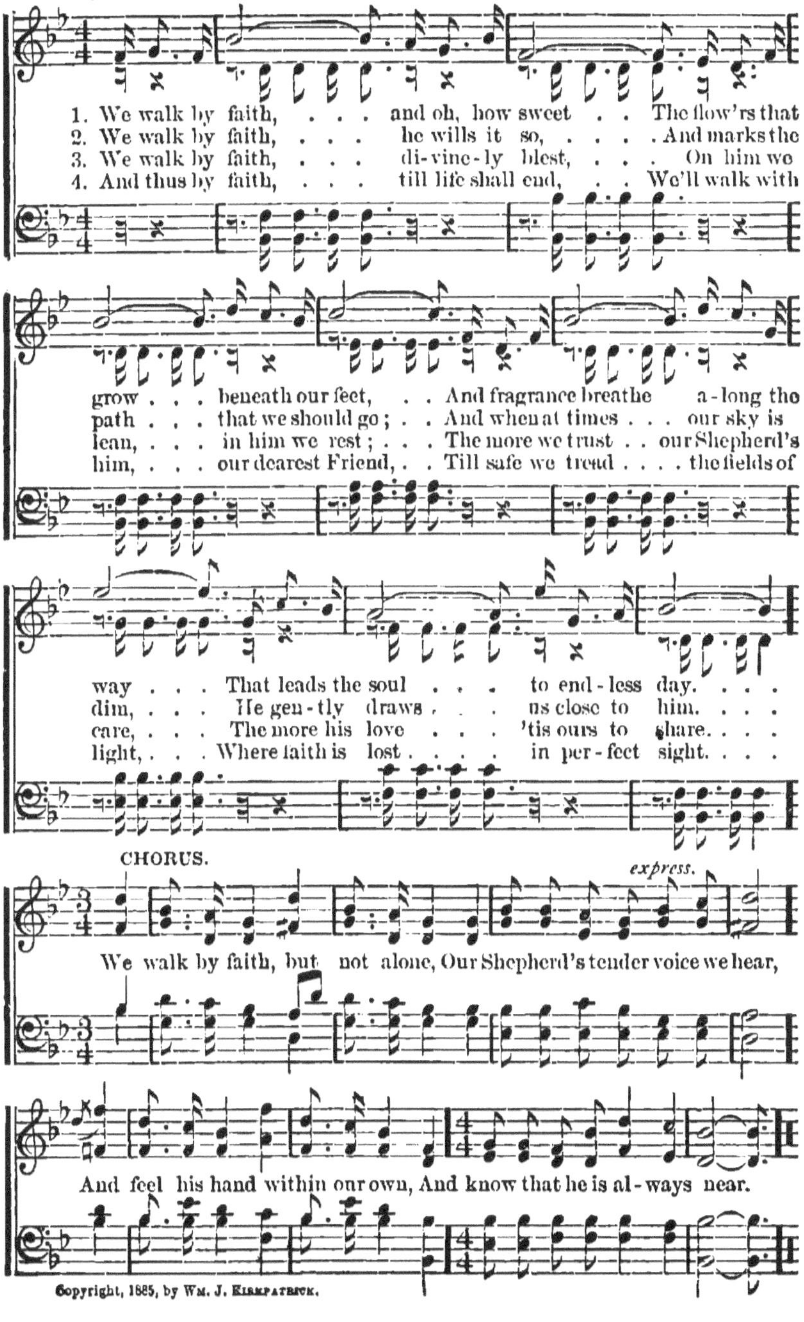

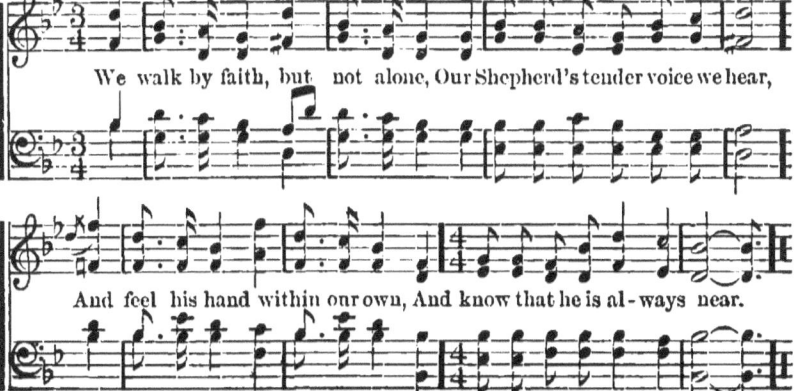

On to Victory.

195

JENNIE WILSON. "This is the victory that overcometh the world." 1 John v: 4. JNO. R. SWENEY.

1. "On to vic-to-ry" shall our mot-to be, While we march as soldiers of Christ our Lord; Ne'er shall come defeat when the foe we meet, If for bat-tle or-ders we take God's word. "On to vic-to-ry, on to vic-to-ry," Hear the ringing bat-tle call, "On to vic-to-ry, on to vic-to-ry," Earth shall crown him Lord of all.

2. "On to vic-to-ry," for on Cal-va-ry Je-sus conquered death that our souls might live; Let us trust his name, and his promise claim, In the Christian warfare he'll triumph give.

3. "On to vic-to-ry," till the world is free From the cru-el bondage and blight of sin; Onward, onward press, gaining new success, Stars to shine for-ev-er thro' Je-sus win.

4. "On to vic-to-ry," till those heights we see Where the an-gel arm-ies of Jesus stand, Then with joyous song we shall join the throng, Singing happy praise in the glo-ry-land.

CHORUS.

Copyright, 1893, by Jno. R. Sweney.

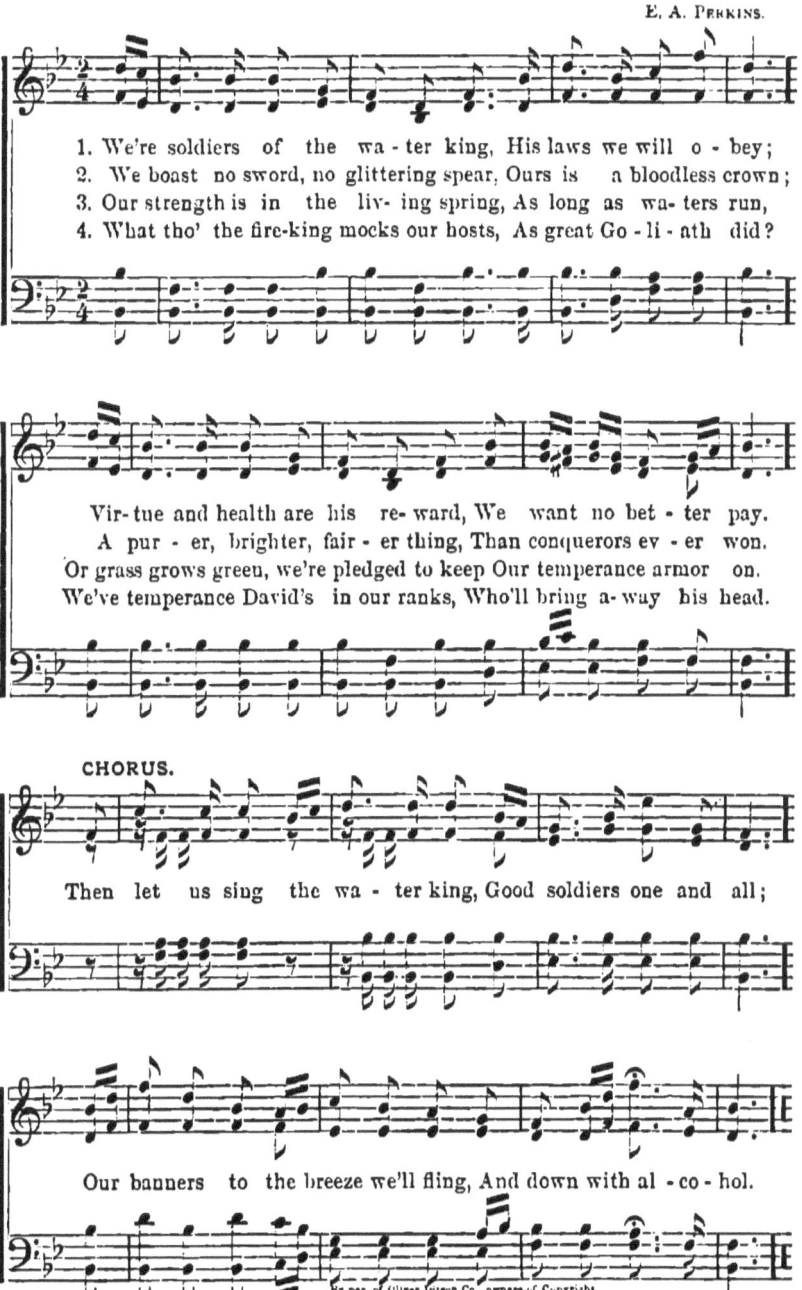

"The Flag."—CONCLUDED.

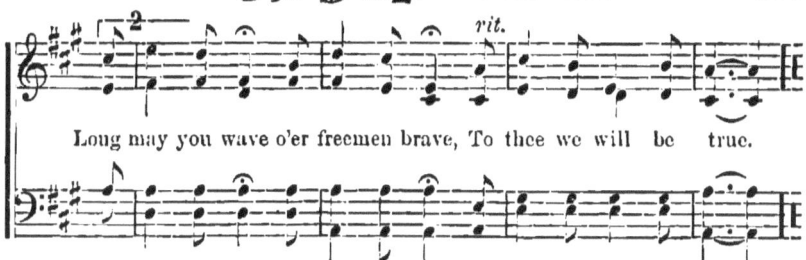

Long may you wave o'er freemen brave, To thee we will be true.

Three Cheers for the Flag.

E. E. HEWITT.   JNO. R. SWENEY.

1. Our banner to the breezes fling, Three cheers for the flag we love; The boys and
2. 'Twas for this flag our fathers fought, Three cheers for the flag we love; Their blood
3. We'll stand for all that's pure and right, [our
   Three cheers for the flag we love; In goodness
4. May peace and plenty crown our land, Three cheers for the flag we love; And may [we

CHORUS.

girls will shout and sing, Three cheers for the flag we love. Hurrah! hurrah! hurrah!
country's freedom bought, Three cheers for the flag we love. [Three
is a nation's might, Three cheers for the flag we love.
know God's guiding hand, Three cheers for the flag we love.

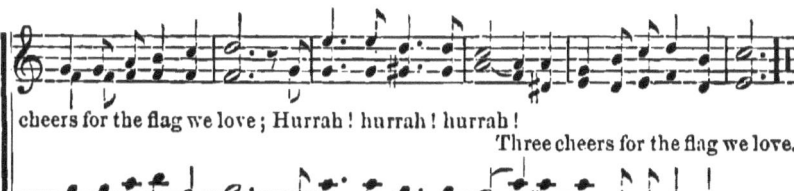

cheers for the flag we love; Hurrah! hurrah! hurrah!
    Three cheers for the flag we love.

Copyright, 1895, by Jno. R. Sweney.

God Keep Us till We Meet Again. 209

"The Lord bless thee and keep thee."—Num. vi: 24.

FANNY J. CROSBY.   W. H. DOANE.

1. God keep us in his ten-der care Till next we meet,
2. God grant the spir-it of his grace To ev-'ry one,
3. God watch between us when our steps May roam a-part,
4. God keep us safe and lead us on Till life is o'er;

And bind in clos-er bonds of love, Our un-ion sweet.
And give us strength to la-bor on Till work is done.
And with his all-sus-tain-ing power Fill ev-'ry heart.
Then bring us home with those we love, To part no more.

REFRAIN.

God keep as now our friendship bright, And hallow its golden chain;
O may not one dear link be missing, When we meet a-gain.

Copyright, 1894, by The Biglow & Main Co. Used by per.

Bless the Lord, my Soul.—CONCLUDED.

for the saving grace, That is so full and free. Bless the Lord, my soul,
for the sense of peace, Amid the surging tide.
for the lov-ing call To worship at his feet.
for the crown of life In thy e-ternal home.

Bless the Lord, my soul; And all that is within me, Bless his ho-ly name.

212. Whate'er it Be.

ELTA M. LEWIS. "Thy will be done." WM. J. KIRKPATRICK.

1. I take my portion from thy hand, And do not seek to understand;
2. When darkness doth thy face obscure, And many sorrows I endure,
3. When tender joys to me are known, I render thanks to thee a-lone;
4. Thus calmly do I face my lot, Accept it, Lord, and doubt thee not;

Cho.—Whate'er it be! whate'er it be! I do not fear, whate'er it be;

D. C. Chorus.

For I am blind, while thou dost see, Thy will is mine, whate'er it be.
I think of Christ's Gethsema-ne; Thy will is mine, whate'er it be.
I know my cup is filled by thee; Thy will is mine, whate'er it be.
Lo! all things work for good to me; Thy will is mine, whate'er it be.

Copyright, 1888, by Wm. J. Kirkpatrick.

Thy love divine sustaineth me, Thy will is mine, whate'er it be.

Antioch. C. M.

213   **O for a thousand tongues.**

1 O FOR a thousand tongues, to sing
   My great Redeemer's praise;
The glories of my God and King,
   The triumphs of his grace!

2 My gracious Master and my God,
   Assist me to proclaim,
To spread through all the earth abroad,
   The honors of thy name.

3 Jesus! the name that charms our fears,
   That bids our sorrows cease;
'Tis music in the sinner's ears,
   'Tis life, and health, and peace.

4 He breaks the power of canceled sin,
   He sets the prisoner free;
His blood can make the foulest clean;
   His blood availed for me.

5 He speaks, and, listening to his voice,
   New life the dead receive;
The mournful, broken hearts rejoice;
   The humble poor believe.

6 Hear him, ye deaf; his praise, ye dumb,
   Your loosened tongues employ;
Ye blind, behold your Saviour come;
   And leap, ye lame, for joy.

214   **Joy to the world!**

1 Joy to the world! the Lord is come;
   Let earth receive her King;
Let every heart prepare him room,
   And heaven and nature sing.

2 Joy to the world! the Saviour reigns;
   Let men their songs employ;
While fields and floods, rocks, hills and
   Repeat the sounding joy.   [plains,

3 No more let sin and sorrow grow,
   Nor thorns infest the ground;
He comes to make his blessings flow
   Far as the curse is found.

4 He rules the world with truth and grace,
   And makes the nations prove
The glories of his righteousness,
   And wonders of his love.

215   **The Lord's Prayer.**

Reverently.

1. Our Father which art in heaven, hallowed | be thy | name, ‖ Thy kingdom come, thy will be done in | earth, as-it | is in | heaven.

2. Give us this day our | daily | bread, ‖ And forgive us our trespasses, as we for- give | them that | trespass a- | gainst us.

3. And lead us not into temptation, but deliver | us from | evil; ‖ For thine is the kingdom, and the power and the | glory for- | ever and | ever. ‖ A- | men.

216. To Us a Child of Hope.

Tune, ZERAH. C. M.

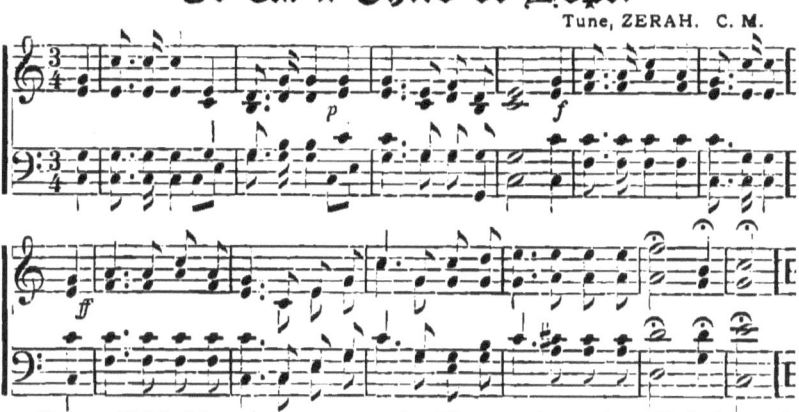

1 To us a Child of hope is born,
  To us a Son is given;
  Him shall the tribes of earth obey,
  Him, all the hosts of heaven

2 His name shall be the Prince of Peace,
  Forevermore adored;
  The Wonderful, the Counselor,
  The great and mighty Lord.

3 His power, increasing, still shall spread;
  His reign no end shall know;
  Justice shall guard his throne above,
  And peace abound below.

4 To us a Child of hope is born,
  To us a Son is given;
  The Wonderful, the Counselor,
  The mighty Lord of heaven.

217. Brightest and Best.

REGINALD HEBER.   Arranged by J. J. H.

1. { Brightest and best of the sons of the morning, Dawn on our darkness and
     Star of the East, the ho-ri-zon a-dorning, Guide where our infant Re-
D. C.—Angels a-dore him, in slumber re-clining,—Maker, and Monarch, and

lend us thine aid: }
deemer is laid.   } Cold on his cradle the dew-drops are shining; Low lies his
Saviour of all.   }

head with the beasts of the stall;

2 Say, shall we yield him, in costly devotion,
  Odors of Edom and offerings divine?
  Gems of the mountain, and pearls of the ocean,
  Myrrh from the forest, and gold from the mine?
  Vainly we offer each ample oblation;
  Vainly with gifts would his favor secure;
  Richer by far is the heart's adoration;
  Dearer to God are the prayers of the poor.

218 Sun of My Soul.

1 SUN of my soul, thou Saviour dear,
  It is not night if thou be near;
  Oh, may no earth-born cloud arise,
  To hide thee from thy servant's eyes.

2 When the soft dews of kindly sleep
  My wearied eye-lids gently steep,
  Be my last thought, how sweet to rest
  Forever on my Saviour's breast.

3 Abide with me from morn till eve,
  For without thee I cannot live;
  Abide with me when night is nigh,
  For without thee I dare not die.

4 Watch by the sick: enrich the poor
  With blessings from thy boundless store;
  Be every mourner's sleep to-night,
  Like infant's slumbers, pure and light.

219 Sing of His Mighty Love.

1 OH, bliss of the purified, bliss of the free,
  I plunge in the crimson tide opened for me;
  O'er sin and uncleanness exulting I stand,
  And point to the print of the nails in his hand.

Cho.—Oh, sing of his mighty love,
 ‖:Sing of his mighty love,:‖
   Mighty to save.

2 Oh, bliss of the purified, Jesus is mine,
  No longer in dread condemnation I pine;
  In conscious salvation I sing of his grace,
  Who lifteth upon me the light of his face.

3 Oh, bliss of the purified, bliss of the pure,
  No wound hath the soul that his blood cannot
     cure;   [rest,
  No sorrow-bowed head but may sweetly find
  No tears but may dry them on Jesus' breast.

4 O Jesus the crucified, thee will I sing,
  My blessed Redeemer, my God and my King;
  My soul filled with rapture shall shout o'er
     the grave,
  And triumph in death in the "Mighty to Save."

220 Revive Thy Work.

1 WE praise thee, O God, for the Son of thy
     love,
  For Jesus who died, and is now gone above.

Cho.—Hallelujah! thine the glory, hallelujah!
   amen;
  Hallelujah! thine the glory, revive us again.

2 We praise thee, O God, for thy Spirit of light!
  Who has shown us our Saviour and scattered our night.

3 All glory and praise to the Lamb that was
     slain,   [every stain.
  Who has borne all our sins, and has cleansed

4 All glory and praise to the God of all grace,
  Who has bought us, and sought us, and
     guided our ways.

5 Revive us again, fill each heart with thy love;
  May each soul be rekindled with fire from
     above.

221 How Sweet the Name.

1 HOW sweet the name of Jesus sounds
    In a believer's ear;
  It soothes his sorrows, heals his wounds,
    And drives away his fear.

2 It makes the wounded spirit whole,
    And calms the troubled breast;
  'Tis manna to the hungry soul,
    And to the weary rest.

3 Jesus, my Shepherd, Saviour, Friend;
    My Prophet, Priest, and King;
  My Lord, my Life, my Way, my End,—
    Accept the praise I bring.

4 I would thy boundless love proclaim
    With every fleeting breath;
  So shall the music of thy name
    Refresh my soul in death.

222 Even Me.

1 LORD, I hear of showers of blessing
    Thou art scattering full and free—
  Showers the thirsty land refreshing;
    Let some droppings fall on me.

Cho.—Even me, even me,
    Let thy blessing fall on me.

2 Pass me not, O gracious Father!
    Sinful though my heart may be;
  Thou might'st leave me, but the rather
    Let thy mercy fall on me.

3 Pass me not, O tender Saviour!
    Let me love and cling to thee;
  I am longing for thy favor;
    Whilst thou'rt calling, oh, call me.

4 Pass me not, O mighty Spirit!
    Thou can'st make the blind to see;
  Witnesser of Jesus' merit,
    Speak the word of power to me.

223 Nearer to Thee.

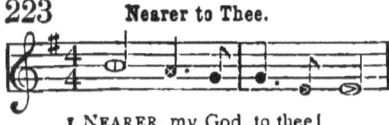

1 NEARER, my God, to thee!
   Nearer to thee,
   E'en though it be a cross
     That raiseth me;
   Still all my song shall be,
   Nearer, my God, to thee,
     Nearer to thee!

2 Though like the wanderer,
     The sun gone down,
   Darkness be over me,
     My rest a stone,
   Yet in my dreams I'd be,
   Nearer, my God, to thee,
     Nearer to thee!

3 There let the way appear,
     Steps unto heaven;
   All that thou sendest me,
     In mercy given;
   Angels to beckon me
   Nearer, my God, to thee,
     Nearer to thee!

224 Fountain.

1 THERE is a fountain filled with blood
     Drawn from Immanuel's veins;
   And sinners, plunged beneath that flood
     Lose all their guilty stains.

2 The dying thief rejoiced to see
     That fountain in his day;
   And there may I, though vile as he,
     Wash all my sins away.

3 Thou dying Lamb! thy precious blood
     Shall never lose its power,
   Till all the ransomed Church of God
     Are saved, to sin no more.

4 E'er since, by faith, I saw the stream
     Thy flowing wounds supply,
   Redeeming love has been my theme,
     And shall be till I die.

225 Coronation.

1 ALL hail the power of Jesus' name!
   Let angels prostrate fall;
   Bring forth the royal diadem,
   And crown him Lord of all.

2 Ye chosen seed of Israel's race,
   Ye ransomed from the fall,
   Hail him who saves you by his grace,
   And crown him Lord of all.

3 Sinners, whose love can ne'er forget
   The wormwood and the gall;
   Go, spread your trophies at his feet,
   And crown him Lord of all.

4 Let every kindred, every tribe,
   On this terrestrial ball,
   To him all majesty ascribe,
   And crown him Lord of all.

5 O that with yonder sacred throng
   We at his feet may fall;
   We'll join the everlasting song,
   And crown him Lord of all.

226 Blest be the tie.

1 BLEST be the tie that binds
     Our hearts in Christian love;
   The fellowship of kindred minds
     Is like to that above.

2 Before our Father's throne
     We pour our ardent prayers;
   Our fears, our hopes, our aims are one,
     Our comforts and our cares.

3 We share our mutual woes,
     Our mutual burdens bear;
   And often for each other flows
     The sympathising tear.

4 When we asunder part,
     It gives us inward pain;
   But we shall still be joined in heart,
     And hope to meet again.

227 How Gentle. Same tune.

1 How gentle God's commands!
     How kind his precepts are!
   Come, cast your burdens on the Lord,
     And trust his constant care.

2 Beneath his watchful eye
     His saints securely dwell;
   That hand which bears all nature up
     Shall guard his children well.

3 Why should this anxious load
     Press down your weary mind?
   Haste to your heavenly Father's throne,
     And sweet refreshment find.

4 His goodness stands approved,
     Unchanged from day to day:
   I'll drop my burden at his feet,
     And bear a song away.

FAMILIAR HYMNS.

228. What a Friend.

1 WHAT a Friend we have in Jesus,
  All our sins and griefs to bear!
What a priveledge to carry
  Everything to God in prayer!
O what peace we often forfeit,
  O what needless pain we bear,
All because we do not carry
  Everything to God in prayer!

2 Have we trials and temptations?
  Is there trouble anywhere?
We should never be discouraged,
  Take it to the Lord in prayer.
Can we find a friend so faithful
  Who will all our sorrows share?
Jesus knows our every weakness,
  Take it to the Lord in prayer.

229. Rock of Ages.

1 ROCK of Ages, cleft for me,
  Let me hide myself in thee;
Let the water and the blood,
  From thy wounded side which flowed,
Be of sin the double cure,
  Save from wrath and make me pure.

2 Could my tears forever flow,
  Could my zeal no languor know;
These for sin could not atone;
  Thou must save, and thou alone;
In my hand no price I bring,
  Simply to thy cross I cling.

3 While I draw this fleeting breath,
  When my eyes shall close in death,
When I rise to worlds unknown,
  And behold thee on thy throne,
Rock of Ages, cleft for me,
  Let me hide myself in thee.

230. Before the Cross.

1 MY faith looks up to thee,
  Thou Lamb of Calvary,
    Saviour divine;
  Now hear me while I pray,
  Take all my guilt away,
  O let me from this day
    Be wholly thine.

2 May thy rich grace impart
  Strength to my fainting heart,
    My zeal inspire;
  As thou hast died for me,
  O may my love to thee
  Pure, warm, and changeless be,—
    A living fire.

3 While life's dark maze I tread,
  And griefs around me spread,
    Be thou my guide;
  Bid darkness turn to day,
  Wipe sorrow's tears away,
  Nor let me ever stray
    From thee aside.

231. Happy Day.

1 O HAPPY day, that fixed my choice
  On thee, my Saviour and my God!
Well may this glowing heart rejoice,
  And tell its rapture all abroad.

Cho.—Happy day, happy day,
  When Jesus washed my sins away;
He taught me how to watch and pray,
  And live rejoicing every day;
Happy day, happy day,
  When Jesus washed my sins away.

2 'Tis done, the great transaction's done—
  I am my Lord's and he is mine;
He drew me, and I followed on,
  Charmed to confess the voice divine.

3 Now rest, my long divided heart;
  Fixed on this blissful centre, rest
Nor ever from thy Lord depart,
  With him of every good possessed.

232. Sweet Hour of Prayer.

1 Sweet hour of prayer, sweet hour of prayer,
  That calls me from a world of care,
And bids me at my Father's throne
  Make all my wants and wishes known!
In seasons of distress and grief
  My soul has often found relief,
And oft escaped the tempter's snare
  By thy return, sweet hour of prayer.

2 Sweet hour of prayer, sweet hour of prayer,
  Thy wings shall my petition bear
To him, whose truth and faithfulness,
  Engage the waiting soul to bless:
And since he bids me seek his face,
  Believe his word, and trust his grace,
I'll cast on him my every care,
  And wait for thee, sweet hour of prayer.

233 Depth of Mercy.

1 DEPTH of mercy! can there be
Mercy still reserved for me?
Can my God his wrath forbear?
Me, the chief of sinners, spare?

Cho.—God is love! I know, I feel;
Jesus lives, and loves me still;
Jesus lives,
He lives and loves me still.

2 I have long withstood his grace,
Long provoked him to his face:
Would not hearken to his calls;
Grieved him by a thousand falls.

3 Now incline me to repent;
Let me now my sins lament;
Now my soul revolt deplore,
Weep, believe, and sin no more.

234 I Hear Thy Welcome Voice.

1 I HEAR thy welcome voice,
That calls me, Lord, to thee,
For cleansing in thy precious blood
That flowed on Calvary.

Cho.—I am coming, Lord,
Coming now to thee!
Wash me, cleanse me in the blood
That flowed on Calvary.

2 Though coming weak and vile,
Thou dost my strength assure;
Thou dost my vileness fully cleanse,
Till spotless all and pure.

3 'Tis Jesus calls me on
To perfect faith and love,
To perfect hope, and peace, and trust,
For earth and heaven above.

4 All hail, atoning blood!
All hail, redeeming grace!
All hail, the gift of Christ our Lord,
Our Strength and Righteousness!

235 The Home Over There.

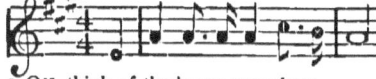

1 OH, think of the home over there,
By the side of the river of light,
Where the saints, all immortal and fair,
Are robed in their garments of white.

Ref.—Over there, over there,
Oh, think of the home over there.

2 Oh, think of the friends over there,
Who before us the journey have trod,
Of the songs that they breathe on the air,
In their home in the palace of God.

Ref.—Over there, over there,
Oh, think of the friends over there.

3 My Saviour is now over there,
There my kindred and friends are at rest;
Then away from my sorrow and care,
Let me fly to the land of the blest.

Ref.—Over there, over there,
My Saviour is now over there.

4 I'll soon be at home over there,
For the end of my journey I see;
Many dear to my heart, over there,
Are watching and waiting for me.

Ref.—Over there, over there,
I'll soon be at home over there.

236 He Leadeth Me!

1 HE leadeth me! O blessed thought!
O words with heavenly comfort fraught!
Whate'er I do, where'er I be,
Still 'tis God's hand that leadeth me.

Cho.—He leadeth me, he leadeth me,
By his own hand he leadeth me:
His faithful follower I would be,
For by his hand he leadeth me.

2 Sometimes 'mid scenes of deepest gloom,
Sometimes where Eden's bowers bloom,
By waters still, o'er troubled sea,—
Still 'tis his hand that leadeth me!

3 Lord, I would clasp thy hand in mine,
Nor ever murmur nor repine,
Content, whatever lot I see,
Since 'tis my God that leadeth me!

237 My Country! 'tis of Thee.

1 MY country! 'tis of thee,
Sweet land of liberty,
Of thee I sing:
Land where my fathers died!
Land of the pilgrims' pride!
From every mountain side
Let freedom ring!

2 My native country, thee,
Land of the noble, free,
Thy name I love;
I love thy rocks and rills,
Thy woods and templed hills:
My heart with rapture thrills
Like that above.

3 Our fathers' God! to thee,
Author of liberty,
To thee we sing;
Long may our land be bright
With freedom's holy light;
Protect us by thy might,
Great God, our King!

238. Saviour, like a Shepherd.

1 SAVIOUR, like a shepherd lead us,
  Much we need thy tend'rest care,
In thy pleasant pastures feed us,
  For our use thy folds prepare;
|: Blessed Jesus, blessed Jesus,
  Thou hast bought us, thine we are. :|

2 We are thine, do thou befriend us,
  Be the Guardian of our way;
Keep thy flock, from sin defend us,
  Seek us when we go astray;
|: Blessed Jesus, blessed Jesus,
  Hear, oh, hear us when we pray. :|

3 Thou hast promised to receive us,
  Poor and sinful though we be;
Thou hast mercy to relieve us,
  Grace to cleanse, and power to free;
|: Blessed Jesus, blessed Jesus,
  We will early turn to thee. :|

239. I Love to Tell the Story.

1 I LOVE to tell the Story
  Of unseen things above,
Of Jesus and his glory,
  Of Jesus and his love;
I love to tell the Story,
  Because I know it's true;
It satisfies my longings,
  As nothing else would do.

Cho.—I love to tell the Story!
  'Twill be my theme in glory,
    To tell the Old, Old Story
      Of Jesus and his love.

2 I love to tell the Story!
  More wonderful it seems,
Than all the golden fancies
  Of all our golden dreams;
I love to tell the Story!
  It did so much for me;
And that is just the reason
  I tell it now to thee.

3 I love to tell the Story!
  For those who know it best
Seem hungering and thirsting
  To hear it, like the rest;
And when, in scenes of glory,
  I sing the NEW, NEW SONG,
'Twill be the OLD, OLD STORY
  That I have loved so long.

240. Jesus, Lover of My Soul.

1 JESUS, lover of my soul,
  Let me to thy bosom fly,
While the nearer waters roll,
  While the tempest still is high.
Hide me, O my Saviour, hide,
  Till the storm of life is past;
Safe into the haven guide,
  O, receive my soul at last.

2 Other refuge have I none;
  Hangs my helpless soul on thee:
Leave, oh, leave me not alone,
  Still support and comfort me:
All my trust on thee is stayed,
  All my help from thee I bring;
Cover my defenceless head
  With the shadow of thy wing!

3 Thou, O Christ, art all I want;
  More than all in thee I find;
Raise the fallen, cheer the faint,
  Heal the sick, and lead the blind.
Just and holy is thy name,
  I am all unrighteousness:
False and full of sin I am,
  Thou art full of truth and grace.

4 Plenteous grace with thee is found,
  Grace to cover all my sin;
Let the healing streams abound;
  Make and keep me pure within.
Thou of life the fountain art,
  Freely let me take of thee;
Spring thou up within my heart,
  Rise to all eternity.

241. There is a Land.

1 THERE is a land of pure delight,
  Where saints immortal reign;
Eternal day excludes the night,
  And pleasures banish pain;
There everlasting Spring abides,
  And never-whith'ring flowers;
Death, like a narrow sea, divides
  This heavenly land from ours.

2 Sweet fields beyond the swelling flood
  Stand dressed in living green;
So to the Jews old Canaan stood,
  While Jordan rolled between;
Could we but climb where Moses stood,
  And view the landscape o'er, [flood
Not Jordan's stream, nor death's cold
  Should fright us from the shore.

242 Come, We that Love.

1 Come, we that love the Lord,
And let our joys be known;
Join in a song with sweet accord,
And thus surround the throne.

2 The men of grace have found
Glory begun below:
Celestial fruits on earthly ground
From faith and hope may grow.

3 The hill of Zion yields
A thousand sacred sweets,
Before we reach the heavenly fields,
Or walk the golden streets.

4 Then let our songs abound,
And every tear be dry; [ground
We're marching through Immanuel's
To fairer worlds on high.

243 O for a Faith.

1 O for a faith that will not shrink,
Though pressed by every foe,
That will not tremble on the brink
Of any earthly woe!

2 That will not murmur nor complain
Beneath the chastening rod,
But, in the hour of grief or pain,
Will lean upon its God;

3 A faith that keeps the narrow way
Till life's last hour is fled,
And with a pure and heavenly ray
Illumes a dying bed.

4 Lord, give us such a faith as this,
And then, whate'er may come,
We'll taste, e'en here, the hallowed bliss
Of an eternal home.

244 Forever Here my Rest.

1 Forever here my rest shall be,
Close to thy bleeding side;
This all my hope and all my plea,
For me, the Saviour died.

2 My dying Saviour and my God,
Fountain for guilt and sin,
Sprinkle me ever with thy blood,
And cleanse and keep me clean.

3 Wash me and make me thus thine own,
Wash me and mine thou art:
Wash me, but not my feet alone,—
My hands, my head, my heart.

4 Th' a-tonement of thy blood apply,
Till faith to sight improve;
Till hope in full fruition die,
And all my soul be love.

245 In the Cross of Christ.

1 In the cross of Christ I glory,
Tow'ring o'er the wrecks of time;
All the light of sacred story
Gathers 'round its head sublime.

2 When the woes of life o'ertake me,
Hopes deceive, and fears annoy,
Never shall the cross forsake me;
Lo! it glows with peace and joy.

3 When the sun of bliss is beaming
Light and love upon my way,
From the cross the radiance streaming
Adds more lustre to the day.

4 Bane and blessing, pain and pleasure
By the cross are sanctified;
Peace is there, that knows no measure,
Joys that through all time abide.

5 In the cross of Christ I glory, etc.

246 My Jesus, I Love Thee.

My Jesus, I love thee, I know thou art mine,
For thee all the follies of sin I resign;
My gracious Redeemer, my Saviour art thou,
If ever I loved thee, my Jesus, 'tis now.

2 I love thee because thou hast first loved me,
And purchased my pardon on Calvary's tree;
I love thee for wearing the thorns on thy brow;
If ever I loved thee, my Jesus, 'tis now.

3 I will love thee in life, I'll love thee in death,
And praise thee as long as thou lendest me
breath; [my brow,
And say, when the death-dew lies cold on
If ever I loved thee, my Jesus, 'tis now.

4 In mansions of glory and endless delight
I'll ever adore thee in heaven so bright;
I'll sing with the glittering crown on my brow,
If ever I loved thee, my Jesus, 'tis now.

247. The Morning Light.

SAMUEL F. SMITH. Tune, WEBB. 7, 6.

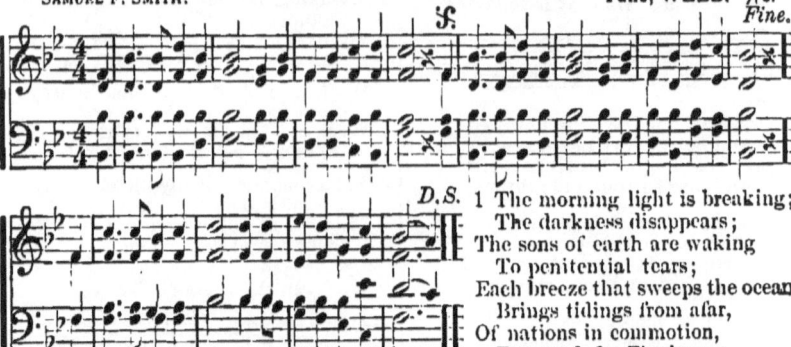

1 The morning light is breaking;
   The darkness disappears;
   The sons of earth are waking
   To penitential tears;
   Each breeze that sweeps the ocean
   Brings tidings from afar,
   Of nations in commotion,
   Prepared for Zion's war.

2 See heathen nations bending
   Before the God we love,
   And thousand hearts ascending
   In gratitude above;
   While sinners, now confessing,
   The gospel call obey,
   And seek the Saviour's blessing,
   A nation in a day.

3 Blest river of salvation,
   Pursue thine onward way;
   Flow thou to every nation,
   Nor in thy richness stay:
   Stay not till all the lowly
   Triumphant reach their home:
   Stay not till all the holy
   Proclaim, "The Lord is come!"

248. Stand up, stand up for Jesus.

GEO. DUFFIELD, Jr.   Tune above.

1 STAND up, stand up for Jesus,
   Ye soldiers of the cross;
   Lift high his royal banner,
   It must not suffer loss;
   From victory unto victory
   His army shall he lead
   Till every foe is vanquished
   And Christ is Lord indeed.

2 Stand up, stand up for Jesus,
   The trumpet call obey;
   Forth to the mighty conflict,
   In this his glorious day:
   "Ye that are men, now serve him,"
   Against unnumbered foes:
   Your courage rise with danger,
   And strength to strength oppose.

3 Stand up, stand up for Jesus,
   Stand in his strength alone;
   The arm of flesh will fail you;
   Ye dare not trust your own:
   Put on the gospel armor,
   Each piece put on with prayer;
   Where duty calls, or danger,
   Be never wanting there.

4 Stand up, stand up for Jesus,
   The strife will not be long;
   This day the noise of battle,
   The next the victor's song:
   To him that overcometh,
   A crown of life shall be;
   He with the King of glory
   Shall reign eternally.

249. Work, for the night is coming.

Key F.

1 WORK, for the night is coming,
   Work through the morning hours;
   Work, while the dew is sparkling,
   Work 'mid springing flowers;
   Work, when the day grows brighter,
   Work in the glowing sun;
   Work, for the night is coming,
   When man's work is done.

2 Work, for the night is coming;
   Work through the sunny noon;
   Fill brightest hours with labor;
   Rest comes sure and soon.
   Give every flying minute
   Something to keep in store;
   Work for the night is coming,
   When man works no more.

3 Work for the night is coming,
   Under the sunset skies;
   While their bright tints are glowing,
   Work, for daylight flies.
   Work till the last beam fadeth,
   Fadeth to shine no more;
   Work while the night is darkening,
   When man's work is o'er.

INDEX.

Titles in CAPITALS; First lines in Roman type.

	HYMN.		HYMN.		HYMN.
ABIDING,	36	BUILDING DAY BY D.	144	HEAVENLY MUSIC,	58
A Christian band	108			HE IS MINE, I AM HIS	90
Again within the h.	129	Children of the morn-	57	He leadeth me,	236
A HUNDRED YEARS	205	Come, we that love	242	HE'LL MENTION	183
A LITTLE TALK,	190	Come, ye weary and.	49	He'll mention them	183
A little talk with Je-	169	Conquering now and	180	HELP JUST A LITTLE	114
ALL-ATONING BLOOD,	122	CONSECRATION,	105	Here in thy name we	175
All for Jesus, all	109			HE SAVES,	47
All hail our country's	204	Depth of mercy,	283	HE TOOK MY PLACE,	71
All hail the power of	225	Down at the cross,	23	HIDE MY SOUL,	55
All my life long	30	Down at the cross, on	10	Hold on, my soul,	99
All praise to him	92	Do you hear that gen-	135	Holy, holy, holy,	181
Amid the trials which	33			Holy, holy, holy Lord	203
Another year has p..	153	Enthroned is Jesus,	18	HOME AT LAST,	120
Anything that Jesus	56	Ev'ry day my soul is	198	Hover o'er me Holy	163
Are we sowing, with	117			How gentle God's c..	227
Are you happy in the	188	FAIR PORTALS,	69	How sweet the name	221
A trembling soul	71	FILL ME NOW,	163		
AT THE CROSS I'LL	88	FOLLOW ALL THE W.	157	I am saved in Christ.	62
At the sounding of	140	Forever here my rest	244	I am saved, the.	17
Awake, O Zion's d.	41	Friends, good night!	208	I do not ask to choose	177
Away beyond the s..	130	FROM HOUSE TO H.	173	If any man thirst, the	150
				I have heard my Sav-	157
BEAUTIFUL ROBES,	156	GLORIA PATRI,	1-3	I have laid my bur-	52
Beautiful star of	5	Glory be to the Fa-	1-3	I hear thy welcome	234
Behold an Israelite in	176	GLORY TO HIS NAME,	23	I hope to meet you	37
Behold a stranger at	154	God keep us in	209	I know that my Re-	151
Behold me standing	70	God loved the world.	46	I love to tell the story	239
BEULAH LAND,	178	GOD'S HOLY CHURCH	136	I'm but a stranger,	9
Blessed assurance, Je-	168	GOD SO LOVED THE W.	46	I'M FREE,	129
BLESSED BE THE NA.	92	GOOD NEWS,	98	I'M LIVING IN CA-	73
Blessed Lily of the V.	90	Go on, go on, ye souls	14	IMMANUEL'S LAND,	21
BLESSED LORD, TAKE	88	Go, ye workers in	173	I must have the Sav-	51
Blessed refuge of the	159			In a world so full of.	115
BLESS THE LORD MY	211	HAPPY IN THEE,	54	In a world where sor-	118
Blest be the tie.	226	Hark the song of holy	120	In the cross of Christ	245
BREAK FORTH IN A S.	4	Hark, the voice of J.	161	IN THE GLORY LAND,	103
Brightest and best of	217	HARVEST TIME.	61	In the good old way	119
BRIGHTEST DAY,	153	HAVE A LITTLE TALK	97	IN THE HOLLOW OF	62
Brother for Christ's k.	114	HEALING FOR THEE,	200	In the hush of	34
BROTHER, WILL YOU	130	HEAVEN IS MY HOME	9	IN THE MASTER'S N.	117

IN THE MORNING, . 42	MARCHING ON TO CA- 48	OPEN THE DOOR, . 125
In the way cast up . 191	Master the tempest is 28	O THAT BEAUTIFUL L. 64
In vain, in high, and 113	MEET ME THERE, . 60	O the great love the . 19
I sang one day, . . 16	'Mid the toil and the 166	O think of the home 235
I take my portion . 212	MISPAH, . . . 85	Our banner, to the . 207
IT MUST BE TOLD, . 152	More about Jesus w.. 63	Our Father, which . 215
I used to think. . 73	MY BARK IS SAFE, . 91	Over the river they . 134
I've reached the land 178	My body, soul, and s. 105	O where will be . 205
I've wandered far a-. 189	My country, 'tis of . 237	
I will go, . . . 89	My faith looks up to. 230	Plant roses, . . 68
I WILL SHOUT HIS . 98	My Father is rich in. 87	PLEADING WITH . 95
	My fragile bark no . 91	Praise God, from w. 1
Jerusalem, thy man-. 11	My Jesus, as thou w. 89	Press on, press on, ye 136
JESUS CAME TO LIVE 131	My Jesus, I love thee 246	
Jesus for me, . . 184	My Saviour first of all 138	REMEMBERED BLESS- 16
Jesus gives his peace 15	My soul for light . 36	REST, . . . 25
Jesus is the light, . 12	My soul in sad exile : 170	Rest ever with God, . 14
Jesus is waiting . 94	My soul is rejoicing . 54	RESTING AT THE C. . 139
JESUS LEADS, . . 192	My soul sings glory . 183	REST, QUIET REST, . 80
Jesus, lover of my s. 240		Ring out a song of g. 179
JESUS, MY JESUS, . 165	NATIONAL SONG, . 204	RING, RING THE B. . 202
Jesus my Saviour is . 184	Nearer, my God, to . 223	Ring the merry C. . 202
Jesus, my Saviour, w. 155	NEARER TO THEE, . 167	Rock of Ages, cleft . 229
JESUS NOW IS CALL-. 49		
JESUS, THE LIGHT, . 93	O brother, have you . 164	SAFE IN THE GLORY . 119
Jesus, the loving . 20	O'er the rapid stream 64	SAFE WITHIN THE V. 35
Jesus, the Saviour, is 125	O for a faith . . 243	SALVATION'S RIVER, . 10
Jesus the Saviour is p. 200	O for a thousand . 213	SANCTUS, . . . 203
JESUS WILL WEL- . 134	Oft I seem to hear . 58	SATISFIED, . . 30
Joy to the world, . 214	O happy day, that . 231	Satisfied by and by, . 18
JUST AHEAD, . . 166	Oh, bless the Lord w. 127	Saviour, lead me, . 78
	Oh, b. the Lord, my . 211	Saviour, like a shep-. 238
KEEP CLOSE TO JESUS 79	Oh, bliss of the . 219	Scattering precious s. 43
Keep thy faith steady 53	Oh, I often sit and . 8	SCATTER SUNSHINE, . 118
	OH, RALLY ROUND . 65	SEND A CHEER ACROSS 147
Land ahead? . . 35	Oh, sometimes the . 31	SEND ME, . . . 161
LEAD ME, SAVIOUR, . 78	Oh, spread the tidings 112	Send out the sunlight 111
LEANING ON THE EV- 171	OH, SUCH WONDER- . 19	SHALL I TURN BACK? 75
Let my gaze be, . 93	Oh, think of the . 235	Shall we meet beyond 128
LET THE SAVIOUR IN 160	Oh, to be like him . 27	SHOWERS OF BLESS-. 175
Let us ask the . . 85	Oh, what a sinner . 131	Simply trusting every 45
LET US HEAR YOU . 164	Oh, why should we . 146	Sing glory to God, . 47
Light after darkness 137	O Jesus Saviour . 88	Sing on, ye joyful . 76
Like a bird on . . 74	O mourner in Zion . 210	Softly and tenderly J. 50
Like an army we are 40	O my Saviour, thou . 122	SOLDIERS OF THE W. 201
Like a shepherd, ten- 192	Only a beam of sun-. 84	Source of life's . . 55
Listen to the still, . 194	Only a little while . 143	Sowing to the spirit, . 66
Living for the Master 199	Only a little word . 44	Speed away! speed a- 107
Lord I hear of show- 222	Only a look from . 80	Standing on the p. . 82
LORD, I'M COMING H. 189	ONLY BELIEVE, . . 146	Stand up, stand up . 248
Lost, lost on the . 75	On the happy golden 60	STAR OF PROMISE, . 5
LOVE IMMORTAL, . 174	On the mount of won- 110	STAY NOT, . . . 94
Love there is that pas- 174	ON THE WAY, . . 127	STEP OUT ON THE P.. 210
LOVINGLY, TENDER-. 20	On to victory shall . 195	STEPPING IN THE L. . 158
	ONWARD AND UP- . 126	Sun of my soul, . 218
MAKE ME A BLESSING 177	Onward, Christian s. 186	SUNSHINE IN THE S.. 106
MARCHING IN THE K. 191	Onward still, and up- 126	Sweet assurance, . 102

HYMN SONGS.

Sweet hour of prayer	232	The still, small v.	194	We are building on	67
Sweetly now are an-.	103	The stranger at	154	We are drifting	81
Swing back for one	69	The summer long	132	We are marching on-	48
		The sure founda-	24	We are nearing,	81
Tell it out with G.	188	The whole wide w.	32	We are pilgrims look-	42
Tell the world of Je-	185	They are pushing out	147	Weary, oh, yes.	95
That gentle whis-.	135	Thine, forever thine,	26	We have been toiling	148
The beautiful l.	12	Tho' dark the night.	190	Welcome for me,	74
The Bethlehem s..	172	Thou thinkest, L.	33	We praise thee,	220
The blessed Nazar-	176	Tho' your sins be as.	182	We're soldiers of the	201
The child of a K..	87	Three cheers for.	207	We shall walk with.	156
The Comforter has	112	Thro' this wilderness	83	We walk by faith	193
The earth is the	4	'Tis a sweet and ten-	152	What a fellowship,	171
The Endeavor B.	108	'Tis the Saviour who	160	What a friend we	228
The flag, the flag,	206	'Tis well,	7	What a gathering	140
The fountain now.	59	To-day God is telling	86	Whate'er it be,	212
The future,	8	Toiling for thee,	148	What rapturous s.	172
The haven of rest,	170	To the cross of C.	139	What will you do.	104
The home where e.	116	To the summer land.	132	When dark and d.	97
The Lord's prayer	215	Touch my spirit	25	When doubts and c..	167
The morning draw-	65	To us a child of hope	216	When he shall c.	197
The morning light	247	Triumph by and by	124	When my life work	138
The new Jerusa-	11	True and faithful	198	When our ships have	22
The new song,	162	Trusting Jesus,	45	When shall we all m.	141
Then rejoice, all.	13	Trying to walk in the	158	When the curtains	142
The Prince of P.	133	'Twas a night of long	133	When the march of	96
The prize is set.	124			When you start for	79
There are songs, glad	187	Use me, O my	101	While the years	115
There are songs of joy	162	Use me, Saviour,	101	Whisper to me,	155
There is a fountain 59,	224	Up with the morn-	128	Who died for me on.	165
There is a land.	241			Will you meet me	6
There's a blessing	52	Valley of Eden,	100	With Jesus,	196
There's a hand held	72	Valley of rest,	100	Wonderful love	113
There's rejoicing in	13	Victory through G.	180	Wonderful peace,	15
There's sunshine in	106			Wonderful story.	86
There stands a Rock.	24	Wait and murmur.	116	Wonderful tidings b.	38
The Rock that is	31	Walking in the l..	199	Wondrous glory,	110
The roll call,	96	Walking with Jesus h	196	Wondrous the favor	197
The sands of time	21	Walking with Jesus m	121	Work, for the night	249
The Saviour with	51	Wash me, O Lamb of	145		
The seed I have scat-	61	We are building in s.	144	You ask what makes	98

www.ingramcontent.com/pod-product-compliance
Lightning Source LLC
Chambersburg PA
CBHW031813230426
43669CB00009B/1130